Symphony
of Spirits

Symphony of Spirits

ENCOUNTERS WITH THE

SPIRITUAL DIMENSIONS

OF ALZHEIMER'S

Deborah A. Forrest, Ph.D.,
with Clint Richmond

St. Martin's Press New York

www.stmartins.com

Book design by Donna Sinisgalli

Library of Congress Cataloging-in-Publication Data

Forrest, Deborah A.
   Symphony of spirits : encounters with the spiritual dimensions of
Alzheimer's/
Deborah A. Forrest, with Clint Richmond.—1st ed.
      p. cm.
   ISBN 0-312-24101-1
      1. Alzheimer's disease—Religious aspects. 2. Dementia—
Religious aspects. 3. Spiritual life. I. Richmond, Clint. II. Title.

RC523 .F67 2000
616.8'31—dc21   00-040260

First Edition: November 2000

1   3   5   7   9   10   8   6   4   2

This book is dedicated
to the memory of my grandfather James Lamar Bird
and my cousin Amelia McConnell Phelps,
the two people who taught me to love, honor,
and listen to the wisdom of my elders;

to the Grandmothers of the Cherokee and Seminole
Nations and the gifts of wisdom they bestowed on their
children's children;

and to the many Alzheimer's patients and family members
who shared their lives and precious time with me.

—DEBORAH A. FORREST, PH.D.

Acknowledgments

This book would not have happened without the encouragement and support of many people who stayed with me throughout the years it took to get it into print. It is with profound gratitude and the deepest appreciation that I acknowledge their contributions—both those here and those in the hereafter.

Thank you, Anne Frankland of Beckenham, Kent, England, for all of your efforts to get this book into print. I will always cherish the tutelage on the publishing business you gave to me so freely. Thank you, Jim Hornfischer, for being such a great literary agent and for introducing me to Bob Weil, the man who made everything begin to happen. Judith Morison, thank you many times over for your brilliant editorial talents and your ability to finesse the challenges of the manuscript rewriting process. Thank you, Julia Pastore, for all of your enthusiasm for this book and your guidance. I am honored to have had the privilege of working with such a fine editor.

Beyond the many talented and brilliant publishing professionals I was fortunate enough to work with on this book are the many family members and friends who were around—both near and far—to give me support and encouragement throughout this long process. I cherish every one of them and their kind words and deeds. Thank you, Becky Ward (for holding your big sister's hand), Richie Ward, Melissa, Madison, and Brandon Trammell, Brian Forrest, Virginia Forrest, Ann and Jim Vest, Bobby Denton, Shirley Janney, Dr. Linda Calvert, Dr. Elisabeth Kübler-Ross, Dr. Catherine Sanders, Dr. Linda Blazina, Dr. Becky Jandrey, Dr. Mary Kingston, Pam L. Morgan, David Railey, Dr. Frederick A. Schmitt, Jeff Howe, Marie Smart, Paul Thompson, Dr. Thomas E. Will, Dr. Patricia White McClanahan, Rev. Mary Storm, Rev. Adei Greenpastures, Lillee Gelinas, and Olga Domin. Finally, to Michael Domin, whose ongoing support and encouragement over these past years allowed me the freedom to write this story, thank you from the bottom of my heart. I couldn't have done it without you.

It is very important for me to also acknowledge the many elders who have crossed over into the spirit world. Their contributions to my life made this part of the journey much easier. My heartfelt appreciation goes to the souls of the people whose stories are told on the pages that follow; and to the souls of Anna Belle, Agatha, Mary, and William "Buddy" Bird; Lowell Forrest and Lilly Forrest Graham; Bill and Jane Lee Forrest Martin; John and Lilly Parker Forrest; Margaret Ruth Hamilton Bird; Elaine Brown; the early 1960s residents of Asbury Acres Nursing Home, Maryville, Tennessee; Dr. Robert Hughes; Dr. William McKenzie; Dr. Thomas Tidmore; and Dr. Inge Broverman.

Contents

Symphony
of Spirits

Introduction

THE EXTRAORDINARY EVENTS described in this book happened to me in the early 1990s, during a two-year nursing contract at a unique geriatric medical facility in a major city in the South. At that facility I was fortunate to work with three dedicated career nurses, who were also steeped in the rich traditions of their Native American and Afro-Caribbean cultures. I was assigned to care for a group of aged patients who, despite their seeming debilitation from dementia, still had much to offer. The names of the hospital staff and patients have been changed, to respect their privacy.

For years I kept their stories locked away in a journal, fearful that people would think I had lost touch with reality if I ever dared speak about them. They would have remained hidden there forever, had it not been for a series of encounters with a group of Alzheimer's patients and their families during my postdoctoral fellowship in aging at a prominent Alzheimer's Disease Research Center in the late 1990s.

During my rotation through the Memory Disorders Clinic, family members of the Alzheimer's patients assigned to me began inquiring about my belief in the existence of spirits. Surprised by these questions, I pressed them for more details about their unusual experiences.

Time and again I heard stories about encounters with the spirits of deceased relatives by the family members and by the Alzheimer's patients themselves. Hearing that Alzheimer's *patients* were "seeing things" was not so unusual to me. After all, I knew from my prior experiences caring for demented patients and from my postdoctoral training that hallucinations are associated with the advanced stages of Alzheimer's disease in some patients. But hearing that *relatives* of the patients were seeing things was completely unexpected.

The people relaying these stories sounded credible. They were all reputable, upstanding, active members of their communities. All were reluctant to talk about the event. I sensed they were fearful of how I would respond. Once comfortable that I would not summon the men with the straitjackets, they spoke freely. Their experiences, in many ways, resembled my own, the ones I have described in this book.

When I learned that others living and working around Alzheimer's patients and other demented elders were having phenomenal experiences, I became more willing to discuss subjects that may be considered controversial by some readers.

I have relied heavily on the nontraditional concepts shared by my Native American, Caribbean, and Afro-American coworkers to explain the often strange and always wondrous things I observed and relay in these stories. I present the unique beliefs they bring from their cultures without judgment of Western bias, because these women, and their roles in what I came to observe, are an integral part of these stories. These women took the concept of a birth-life-death-rebirth cycle and made it real for me. They taught me that this cycle has been an important part of the belief systems of many indigenous populations around the world for thousands of years and that it can be just as meaningful in today's modern society.

In most Native American cultures, a bond of trust must be built before any discussions of the spirit world can ever take place. By first sharing some information about myself and my journey from a small Smoky Mountain town to a large metropolitan geriatric hospital, I want the reader to understand that I consider myself an ordinary person who has been given an opportunity to experience a series of remarkable events involving a spiritual dimension.

In our Appalachian Mountain culture where elders were revered for their wisdom, growing up among the elderly seemed natural to me. Stories about local areas being inhabited by spirits and tales of wise old women seers living in the mountains were commonplace.

My parents were well into their middle years by the time my sisters and I came along. My father's hair was already white when I was born. My sisters and I were raised in a small east Tennessee valley town, surrounded by relatives already in their golden years. We had aunts and uncles who were old enough to be our grandparents, cousins as old as our parents, and a paternal half sister old enough to be our mother.

As a child, I seemed to have a gift for "knowing what was in people's souls." My mother, who also manifested that visionary sensitivity, did not encourage me in this and warned me against using it. When I persisted in talking to her about the unspoken things I sensed in other people, she scolded me. I think it was because she had resisted her own prescience and knew what kind of trouble that sort of thing could get a girl into in a good Protestant community like Maryville, Tennessee, my hometown.

When I was about eight years old, my mother finally put her foot down about my "seeing into people's souls."

"Don't talk about these kinds of things any more," she admonished. "People will think you're crazy. They will lock you up."

I turned my attention to more practical matters. I focused on doing schoolwork, helping my maternal grandfather build things and tend to his rose garden, and learning skills such as sewing and public speaking from Amelia, one of my mother's elderly cousins. It would be nearly forty years before I dared to acknowledge to myself or anyone else that I possessed any extrasensory perceptive abilities. Even now I still have difficulty talking about the "spirit information" I pick up when I'm around people.

Being surrounded by aging parents and elderly relatives during our formative years forced my sisters and me to face the fragility of life at an early age. But these life lessons were difficult to accept when, in the mid-1970s, a series of deaths began to claim too many members of my immediate family. My seventy-one-year-old father was the first to pass away unexpectedly, shortly after my twenty-second birthday. Within eighteen months, his eldest daughter, my fifty-year-old half sister, died. Just one year later, my mother succumbed to a massive heart attack at the age of sixty.

Coping with the overwhelming pain of so many deaths falling so close together while I was still in my early twenties was nearly impossible. Trying to provide emotional support to my sisters, while working full-time to support myself financially, complicated my grief process. I found some solace in my college course work. I was within a few credits of completing an undergraduate degree in nursing when my mother passed away. To be the first female in my family to get a college degree was a goal I had set for myself when I graduated four years earlier from St. Mary's Hospital Nursing School in Knoxville, Tennessee, in 1971. I used that goal to help me build a bridge from the pain of the past to hope for the future.

I developed coping strategies, which included limiting my time around old people, avoiding all funerals—even those of extended family members I loved—and focusing on developing a career in healthcare. For the next fifteen years my goals included completing undergraduate and graduate programs in nursing and achieving success in a variety of clinical and corporate healthcare positions throughout the South and Southwest. Once these were accomplished, I discovered that my choices in life between the mid-1970s and the mid-1980s had distanced me from the memories of those painful losses that had come so close together.

In 1985 I left nursing to become a consultant for a group of medical-device manufacturers. My nursing expertise paid off in the corporate world, and I rarely had to go near a hospital or a dying patient. I was earning a living on the periphery of medicine without having to make the emotional commitments that day-to-day patient caregiving required.

Even as I tried to avoid emotional involvement, I had a powerful experience that foreshadowed the events that would happen later in my life. In 1986 my only living uncle was diagnosed with an advanced case of metastatic lung cancer. He succumbed to the cancer's rapid destruction within just a few months.

Uncle Buddy's former wife wanted to bury him in a cemetery she had selected for the two of them while they were still married.

A short time before he died, my uncle whispered to me that he wanted to be buried, instead, with the rest of his relatives in an old church cemetery in the foothills of the Smoky Mountains. I made sure his wish was granted.

Since Buddy was the last elder of my mother's family, I felt obligated to attend his funeral. None of the excuses I had used in the past would work. During the graveside service, while everyone else was listening to the minister give his final words of comfort to the family, I experienced an unusual intuitive or extrasensory event. As we all stood in the glaring sunlight of the late August summer afternoon, I sensed or perceived that I was hearing the voices of my deceased grandparents and their children, my Uncle Buddy and my mother. They were all thanking me for finally bringing their family back together again in the spirit world.

Even though I was shaken to the very core of my soul by this event, I remained silent about it. In my efforts to understand what had happened to me that day in the cemetery, I resorted to a pattern of behaviors that years of academic training had taught me to use for getting answers to unknown questions. I began extensive research into the scientific literature on the paranormal. This search, independent of any academic program, eventually led me to material on shamanism and its discussions of the spirit world.

Shamanism, in its many religious and cultural forms and in different parts of the world, predates written history. It is a mystical or spiritual way of looking at life and everything—plant, animal, and mineral—that surrounds human existence. Paleontologists have found evidence that shamanism, in its earliest forms, may have even been practiced by Neanderthal people. Shamanic beliefs are still practiced in native cultures in Asia, North and South America, Australia, and Africa. All the original European peoples held their male and female shamans in high esteem, much as we follow the spiritual guidance of our own religious and spiritual leaders today. Shamans are said to have mastered death. The shaman of a tribe or group of people is thought to have powers to heal the sick and communicate with the world beyond.

Native peoples in northern Europe today still practice forms of shamanism, and many people in the so-called industrialized nations still incorporate shamanic beliefs in their daily lives, if not in their organized religions.

I learned that shamanism is a way of looking at the world of the spirits as well as the everyday world around us. One of many approaches used by indigenous groups around the world to make sense of life and its challenges, it encompasses more of the spiritual universe than contemporary traditional Western religions. Shamanism is by no means the only way of gaining an understanding of the spiritual dimension of a person's existence. But for me, it provided a way to look at the totality of life, beyond what our five senses can reveal to us.

Although I was making good money and enjoying the perks of the corporate world, I began to realize something was missing in my life. In 1989 I decided to return to the academic community for a doctoral degree in psychology.

I found an accredited university in Santa Barbara, California, which offered a Ph.D. program for adult midcareer professionals. The program allowed its candidates to complete the course work off campus via a special intranet computer system and independently under the supervision of a local designated faculty coordinator. Such a faculty person was available in a southern city where I had previously worked. I had excellent contacts from my nursing days and knew I could find temporary jobs there while earning this advanced degree. As expected, I easily found plenty of work through temporary placement agencies that specialized in the healthcare field.

When I wasn't in California or involved in the clinical training portion of my Ph.D. program, I worked as a temporary contract nurse. The flexible schedule provided assignments by the day, week, month, or year. In addition to assignments in every psychiatric hospital in the metropolitan area, I worked on numerous medical wards, pushing pills and passing bedpans, and occasionally in an operating room department that was shortstaffed. I covered the whole cross-section of general nursing, a few days at a time.

One of these temporary nursing jobs took me to a unique medical facility unlike any place I had ever worked, which I will call the Plantation. It was a small satellite hospital located immediately adjacent to its huge general-hospital parent complex. The job was in a special geriatric ward, called a gero-neuro-psychiatric unit.

Ironically, my experience at my uncle's graveside and my efforts to understand it using a linear, academic, scientific approach eventually would serve as fodder for my Native American and Afro-Caribbean coworkers at the Plantation, when they began to teach me about shamanism and their understanding of the spirit world.

My unusual experiences and the insights into the shaman realm led me to believe that there is a spiritual dimension to Alzheimer's disease and other progressive, degenerative diseases of aging, a dimension that grows in magnitude as the stricken person's physical mind and body wither. If we dare acknowledge this spiritual dimension in these patients, we will find that they are not lost to us, that they have a valuable gift to offer those who love and care for them.

When I opened my mind and heart, the world as I knew it— my very concept of the cycle of birth, life, death, and the afterlife— was changed forever.

ONE

Plantation of Aging Souls

I HEARD VOICES coming from the private room, but when I entered, I found my patient asleep, and no one else around. After gently closing the door behind me, I went to the foot of the high bed to observe the sleeping figure. I had grown so fond of this woman in the short time she had been under my care. While she apparently was often cantankerous at her nursing home, here at the geriatric hospital she had graced us with a sweet, appreciative disposition when anyone showed her the slightest kindness.

Her breathing was labored, and I decided she must have dozed off just after I heard her voice from the hallway. Then she began to speak again. I thought she was talking in her sleep, but her whispered words were clear and youthful. I listened hard to catch pieces of what she was saying.

"Momma, is that you? Poppa, tell Momma to wait for me. Uncle John . . . Uncle John, can I play just a little longer? Zach . . . Zach . . . tell Momma to take me too! It's my turn to go!"

As I stood frozen, misty figures began to materialize on each side of the bed. They posed beside the frail body, as naturally as thousands of bedside visitors I had seen with patients throughout my nursing career. I was standing within an arm's length of these apparitions. They seemed to pay no attention to my presence.

The old woman continued to talk. Her eyelids fluttered occasionally, as if she were trying to wake up but could not. I sensed that the ethereal visitors were telling her to come along and leave the hospital with them. They seemed to be assuring her that there was a much better option for her than returning to the nursing home, or anything else available to her now.

Suddenly there was a movement on the bed. She was trying to sit up. I saw her clearly, pale and painfully thin, trying to rise. I wanted to go to her but felt glued to the floor. This image of a frail woman struggling to raise herself up while her visitors did nothing was so real that I wanted to shout to them to help her.

Then it struck me. The patient was still lying flat on her back. I could see her through the image of the entity I saw rising up from her in the bed. The pale presence was an identical, watery shadow of the real woman. It was rising from her body and reaching out to the visitors.

My years of training and experience overrode my fascination with what I was seeing. A wave of panic swept through me. My patient was dying. Her spirit was leaving her body.

I shouted for help at the top of my voice. I wanted someone, anyone, to come into the room. The door was closed, so I doubted that any of the other nurses could hear me call out. I rushed to the side of the bed, half expecting to run up against the mysterious visitors. But there was no physical contact, there was nothing, as I reached the spot where the visitors had been only moments before.

Eighteen months earlier, on a beautiful autumn morning, I had driven to a new assignment at a medical facility dedicated to the care of demented old people. The scheduling supervisor at the contract nursing agency had warned that I might not care for this type of temp work.

"Deborah, we've had problems keeping this spot filled," she said on making the assignment. "Most of our nurses prefer to take easier placements."

I did not need to ask why. Elderly people suffering from late-stage neurodegenerative diseases and dementia are among the most challenging patient populations. Many nurses considered caring for these patients to be one of the least desirable jobs in nursing. But I was confident that after some of my other recent and not-so-pleasant assignments, I could handle just about anything—at least for a day or two. I knew, as a contract nurse, I could pretty much decide how long I wanted to stay on this job.

I pulled off the main street onto a winding road arched over by towering trees. The scenic driveway led to the small hospital, nestled amid acres of undeveloped land in near-pristine condition. A hint in the air suggested cooler days would soon be breaking the oppressive grip of an unusually long, hot and humid summer. As I neared the facility, I crossed a bridge over a creek and noticed a large pond on the left side of the road.

I was almost a half-hour early for my scheduled 7 A.M. appointment, the start time for the day shift. The woods and pond were such a pleasant contrast to the asphalt and concrete of the southern metropolitan area, that I pulled off the road to take in the view.

The mist rising off the surface of the pond gave a dreamlike quality to the scene. I got out of the car and walked beneath the willows to a small clearing by the water. From there I could look up the hill to the imposing main hospital building and an assortment of smaller, modern structures.

The buildings and grounds, including assisted-living housing units, were beautifully landscaped and looked nothing like the usually sterile, treeless medical-center complexes.

Waking birds began to chirp and chatter, until the woods were filled with their song. There was no one else in sight—in the woods, on the twisting road, or around the buildings up on the hill. Leaves had already begun to fall, and the only human sound was my own footsteps crunching on the crisp leaf mat of the forest floor.

This little glade would become my frequent stopping place in the seasons to follow: an early-morning chapel where I could prepare myself for the rigors of the day ahead and a late-afternoon refuge to contemplate the extraordinary things I would experience over the next two years.

When I finally drove into the parking lot and saw the colonnaded facade, the facility looked more like a modified antebellum mansion than a hospital. From the front it appeared to be a sprawling one-story building. The elevators inside the lobby—which was invitingly decorated like a stately living room—were the first hint that the building had two or more floors.

My assignment in the gero-neuro-psychiatric unit was on the lower level, which had been bulldozed from the back side of the hill and was not visible from the front of the structure.

The initial job assignment was for only one shift, one day.

I was met at the unit by the night supervisor, the unit's head nurse, and the shift charge nurse. Such a grand reception should have been a clue about how desperate they were for help. However, since I was supposed to be there for only one shift, the night supervisor and the head nurse did not linger after extending a profusely courteous welcome. They immediately left the unit, I assumed for administrative offices somewhere else in the building. I did not see them again on the floor that day and seldom on the unit in the future.

They left me in the capable hands of the day-shift charge nurse, who introduced me around the unit and instructed me on my duties.

She was an unusually strong-looking woman—not tall, about five foot two—but very stout and muscular, with bronze skin and long raven hair. She wore white, soft leather moccasins with her white uniform. When she turned to lead me down the hall, I saw strings of colorful Indian beads braided into her thick black hair.

Her name was Dolly.

As we proceeded down the corridor, she showed me the private and semiprivate rooms for patients, the day room, and a dining area. Frequently during the quick tour she fixed her large doe-shaped black eyes on my face, as if studying my reaction to each person and thing she introduced to me.

Dolly knew the names of every one of the old men and women we encountered, whether they were cases assigned to her or not.

A few of the patients responded to her cheerful greetings with a smile or hello, but most just looked back in vague recognition that someone had called out their name. An old man propelled himself slowly, aimlessly around the unit supported by a walker. Dolly paused long enough to direct him toward the activities section of the day room, but added as we continued on our tour, "He'll be lost again before he reaches the end of the corridor."

Some patients were confined to their beds for medical reasons or because they were simply too debilitated to get out of bed. These people needed assistance with their most basic daily routines.

A few of the patients—mostly men—were sitting in their rooms alone. They were fully dressed but seemed oblivious to their surroundings. They just sat in a corner, staring at the wall.

"Why don't you take them to the day room?" I asked.

"They get upset if we force them to join the others," Dolly answered almost sadly. "They're just waiting."

I started to ask "Waiting for what?" but I didn't want Dolly to have to voice the answer we both already knew.

Once the unit tour was completed, Dolly gave instructions on the special needs of two of my patients and then brusquely answered my technical questions. She seemed to be on guard. Such posturing was common between a permanent hospital staff member and an agency nurse. I knew that only time and a close observation of my skills would erase doubts in the charge nurse's mind about my ability to deliver good care to the patients she had entrusted to me.

It was common practice for a temp nurse from an agency to be assigned the worst patients on any ward or unit. This place was no exception. My initial assignment was to care for eight patients who were bedridden and had to be moved about for medical treatment or other care in wheelchairs or on gurneys. I was told that a nursing assistant or aide was usually available to carry out, or at least help with, many of the unpleasant chores that came with caring for such physically demanding patients. While there was a shortage of aides at the facility, I was fortunate to have a cheerful woman named Nancy assigned to me.

"Think of it this way," Dolly said almost apologetically. "You only have to take care of eight of these old people. There are nearly four million of them with Alzheimer's disease, hidden away in the nooks and crannies of this great country."

"Four million with Alzheimer's?" I was surprised by the statistic.

"Yep, darn near. And that's just one of the degenerative diseases of old age that we see around here," answered Dolly. "There's no shortage of patients in this field, just a shortage of people to take care of them."

She went on to explain that the four million included only those cases that were advanced enough to interfere with the person's activities of daily living. People in earlier stages were never counted in the statistics. And with the country's aging population, that number would continue to grow.

"We haven't made much progress in diagnosing and treating elderly people with diseases that produce dementia," she said. "Most of these old people are still treated like crazy aunts in the attic."

The unit's capacity was twenty-four patients, and I was assigned to care for six women and two men, ranging in age from their late seventies to early nineties.

Of the two dozen patients in this unit, most were suffering from advanced stages of Alzheimer's disease. A patient's admission to the unit was usually prompted by an acute medical or neurological crisis that required immediate attention by a physician.

"Until the Alzheimer's patient enters the final phases of the disease, most are cared for at home or in community-based facilities, such as nursing homes or assisted-living centers," Dolly said.

Although the majority of the patients at the Plantation were in the advanced stages of Alzheimer's, others had diseases such as Huntington's and Parkinson's. These degenerative diseases, in their later stages, have one major characteristic in common: The patients often suffer from progressive dementia, characterized by a slow decline in memory, language, visuospatial skills, personality, and thought.

Dementia is not a disease but a symptom of many diseases, particularly those just mentioned. It can occur at any age—young persons with brain damage due to injury, illness, or drug abuse can suffer symptoms of dementia. But it is most often associated with the diseases of aging.

While dementia may be reversible in some cases of traumatic head injury and nondegenerative illnesses, in Alzheimer's and other degenerative diseases of the elderly, it is a progressive syndrome that results in a persistent decline of intellectual abilities. Patients gradually suffer combinations of disturbed communication skills, loss of memory, loss of cognitive skills, loss of visual and spatial abilities, and, ultimately, loss of control of vital bodily functions.

Along with intellectual impairment, patients may also evidence behavioral or mood changes. Often these symptoms are the first signs that the loved ones of elderly family members recognize. Many patients with dementia also suffer disruptions of normal sleep cycles.

As I started onto the unit to begin my duties that day, Dolly returned to the nurse's station to prepare for the physician rounds that would take place as soon as the doctors arrived on the unit. I took mental note of the unit's routine so I could be as helpful as possible during my time on the job. The activities were considerably different from a regular hospital ward because of the broad array of treatments the patients required, including longer-term care for some, and their varying capacities to function on their own.

Several of the old patients, who were so physically fragile they had to be confined to wheelchairs, were pushed to the day room where they remained parked in front of the TV set until someone came to move them again—either to the dining facility or back to their rooms. Other patients were more mobile and could dress themselves and move about on their own.

The television was the center of activity on the unit for many patients. A cluster of old women and a few old men, some sitting on the chairs and couches facing the set, vacantly stared at whatever was tuned in at the time. Talk shows seemed to be the regular fare.

A few of the patients who were scattered in chairs around the large, sunny room, were reading outdated newspapers and magazines or tattered old books with really large print. Here and there I saw pairs of patients joined in almost whispered conversations.

At mealtime most of the patients were escorted to their seats in the dining area or wheeled up to a table. Several needed assistance in handling their food. All of the staff pitched in to make sure everyone's nutritional needs were fulfilled. Some of the more agile patients even helped the weaker ones get food from the plates to their mouths.

"The meals are very important," Dolly told me as we helped two patients cut up food on their lunch trays. "Getting proper amounts of food and fluids into these folks is as much a part of their treatment as the pills."

In the dining room, Rose, the other staff nurse, briefly joined Dolly and me. She pulled up a chair beside an old woman at our table and began cooing to the patient about what a good girl she was for eating everything on her luncheon menu. The woman did not respond, staring blankly at her empty plate.

"The meals are important for other reasons too," Rose said. "Many of them contain pills that have been crushed up and mixed in with the foods these old folks can swallow. That's the only way a lot of them can get their medications down. They have to take so much medication at a time. I'm twenty-five years younger than any of them, and I know that I couldn't swallow all of the pills they have to down in a given day. Sometimes these old souls at the Plantation just amaze me."

"Plantation? What's that about?" I asked.

"Oh, that's what we affectionately call this place," said Dolly. She puckered her lips as if she had bitten into a lemon. I chuckled, as much at her facial expression as at the strange name for a medical facility.

"Why is that?" I asked, really curious to know. Usually a nickname, particularly one given by the line nurses to a workplace or a doctor, also carried a coded warning that there were problems. Sometimes it is a clue, a sort of gallows humor, masking a serious issue. Even in the South, calling a place a "plantation" had definite overtones.

"If you stick around, you'll see," Dolly replied in such a light-hearted manner that I did not take it too seriously at the time.

As predicted, the longer I extended my assignment, the more I perceived a plantation-like working environment at the place. There was an unspoken but clear distinction between those with some level of power and those with little or none.

The physicians who streamed onto the unit to visit individual patients were from old, aristocratic southern families or northern families with money. I soon realized that quite a number of the patients were also from old aristocratic families along the eastern seaboard. Perhaps, I thought, it was because of the high cost of specialized geriatric care at this facility that it attracted a wealthier clientele.

Another factor in this work environment was the unspoken relationship between some of the patients' families and the immediate caregivers. The families of the patients carted Mama—usually it was Mama, sometimes Papa—off to the hospital. Some patients' relatives had the attitude that the nurses were just servants hired by the hospital to attend to all of their family's demands. I learned that in many of those cases the hospital's administrative staff shared these views and supported the family rather than the staff if a difficulty arose.

In the late 1980s and early 1990s, such treatment of healthcare providers was an anachronism. With the advances nurses had already made in their academic preparation and political status within healthcare, I was quite surprised that we were expected to accept an atmosphere where we were treated like handmaidens and servants from a bygone era reminiscent of the Old South.

The doctors, who came to the facility only once a day unless there was an emergency, were either from private practice or in geriatric training. The rest of the medical staff came from the large parent hospital a quarter of a mile down the road. It was also a fully accredited university teaching hospital.

But while we operated in a veritable thicket of doctors, none came to the unit except when absolutely necessary. Most of the time the front-line staff had complete physical responsibility for the patients.

The same situation existed on the adjoining twenty-four-bed

psychiatric unit adjacent to the neuro-psych unit. Upstairs was a fully equipped medical unit, complete with beds for twenty-two patients, and every form of medical equipment required by geriatric medical specialists to treat the myriad of diseases that afflicted their elderly patients.

Usually twelve to fifteen staff members worked directly with patients during each of the three shifts. The gero-neuro-psych unit where I worked had three staff nurses and two or three assistants to help them. The administrative head nurse on each unit provided no direct patient care.

Any patient who needed special medical services was taken by ambulance or van off the grounds, down the road, and over to the full-service hospital at the university medical center.

Dolly informed me that elderly patients usually were sent to the Plantation because their medical conditions warranted immediate attention, or because they were creating behavioral disturbances that could no longer be managed by their primary caregivers. In some cases, the elderly person had stopped sleeping altogether; after several days with no rest the physical body gave way. Thus, the elder was at medical risk.

"Many nurses just don't want to deal with this population," Dolly said after observing my performance for a few days. "But I think you're doing fine with these old folks."

Though she seemed genuinely impressed with my work, I thought her praise might be exaggerated because of the terrible shortage of nurses in the field of geriatrics. I knew that very few healthcare workers specialized in treating patients with dementia. The situation could only worsen with the rapid growth of the elderly population. Healthcare professionals were giving little thought to how diseases of the aged would assume an increasingly larger place in the epidemiology of America and the rest of the industrialized world.

As I became familiar with the routine at this unusual medical facility, my greatest remaining curiosity was about my coworkers on the day shift.

At first, the three women I worked with daily—Dolly, Rose, and Nancy—had been courteous but almost secretive about themselves. Their coolness toward me quickly thawed when, after a week or ten days coming to work as a temp on a day-to-day basis, I mentioned I would not mind making this assignment semipermanent. It was as if I had accepted them, as if it were a personal compliment. And if truth be known, it was. My observation of the way these unique and talented women handled their difficult patients was a significant factor in my decision to stay at the Plantation for a while. From my first day on the unit I was impressed by the tenderness and the respectful manner with which they treated their patients, even when faced with the most provocative disdain by some of the old-timers.

When I told them I wanted to stay, each woman nodded and beamed at the news. I felt as if I had been voted into the club. I do not know if their eagerness for me to join the staff had been predetermined by management or if it was a consequence of our personal interaction. At the end of each day during that first week or so, I had been asked to come back the next day. During one of our morning coffee breaks, the three women proudly announced that the management at the facility wanted to offer me a contract. Dolly had apparently cleared the offer with the front office.

A contract meant that the hiring institution was willing to make a longer-term arrangement with the temp agency. By that time I had worked on the unit long enough to feel comfortable being surrounded all day by patients in various stages of dementia. So I entered into a three-month contract, which was to be renewed over and over again. A few weeks later I completed the admissions process for my doctoral program. The job provided an ideal schedule, allowing me nights and weekends for study.

We began each day by reviewing the patient reports from the previous two shifts. Next we checked on the patients to see if they were awake and helped those who were able to get out of bed and get ready for the day. The nursing assistants helped the patients who could not move about on their own.

The three women on my shift had made a conscious decision to work with this challenging population. They had one characteristic in common—all claimed at least some link with an ancient native heritage. As is customary in their respective cultural traditions, they required much time before they developed a level of trust in me and before any one of them would share an ounce of personal information with me. But when that trust gradually materialized, what I learned was fascinating.

I first learned a little about my coworkers during rare coffee breaks and stolen moments. Dolly suggested we use those infrequent times when our chores were done and the patients occupied, to get to know each other. She usually invited Rose and Nancy to join us for these morning rituals in a tiny sanctuary tucked behind the nurse's station, appropriately called the break room.

We swapped bits of personal history as we savored a cup of coffee during rest breaks. Dolly was proud that she was from the Cherokee reservation in North Carolina. I said that I had been raised just over the mountains in Tennessee. She was flattered that I knew of her tribe, the Eastern Band of the Cherokee Nation. I hinted at the possibility that I had a touch of Cherokee blood flowing through my own veins.

"Yeah, sure," Dolly teased. "All palefaces want to think they're part Indian—Cher made it chic."

Unlike many Native Americans struggling for success, Dolly had not worked her way off the reservation. The outside world was as much a part of her formative experience as the reservation in North Carolina she called home. Her family was part of a group of Cherokee who lived half of the year on the reservation and the other half in New York City. There the men worked as steeplejacks and high-steel walkers who built and repaired skyscrapers and bridges. These men were said to be fearless as they ran across the cold steel beams and catwalks, because they were part eagle.

Dolly had spent much of her childhood in Manhattan and thus had been exposed to, and educated in, the Western system. The family returned to their home on the reservation in North Carolina each year during the winter months when icy weather conditions prevented them from working. During these winter sojourns, the "grandmothers" took charge of the child's education.

So Dolly had the dual exposure to a Western education and to the wisdom of the ancients. In her childhood years, her roots to her rich tribal heritage were strengthened through her associations with her paternal grandmother and the Cherokee elders still living on the reservation. Even with her Western education and technical nurse's training, she found technology wanting at some basic spiritual level.

She rarely talked about her New York experiences, and it was only by accident that I later discovered she had graduated from nursing school at a prestigious New York medical facility. I also learned she had an undergraduate degree in pre-law from one of the universities in New York City. While her nursing training and the skills she manifested were stellar, I eventually discovered that her roots were deeply embedded in the Cherokee culture.

Dolly was in her early forties. Rose, the other registered nurse on the shift, was in her mid-fifties. Nancy, the nursing assistant who worked with me most of the time, was in her early thirties. While Dolly was forthcoming with information about herself, Rose and Nancy were less willing to share personal details.

Rose had been an RN for more than two decades. She was the only small person on the team, carrying about 130 pounds on her five-feet-five frame. But Dolly frequently assured me that, despite Rose's slight build, she knew how to handle the challenges of dealing with the sometimes hyperactive or even violent patients.

Rose was a descendant of a group of African Americans who had intermingled and married into the Seminole Indian tribes of the Florida Everglades. She was proud of this Native American part of her heritage.

I had read, way back in high school history, of the Seminole Indians and other southern tribes that took in runaway slaves and assimilated them into their tribes. But Rose was the first person from such a historic union of peoples that I had ever met. If she had not told me of her Native American blood and heritage, I would never have guessed at the connection. Her complexion was very light and without wrinkles, making her appear far younger than her actual age.

She was extraordinarily neat, and her white uniform was crisply starched and ironed every day. Rose was just as fastidious with the appearance of the patients in her charge, and she kept their rooms and their persons neat and clean beyond the standard that would normally be required of such a busy nurse.

Rose had been married for more than thirty years and had two grown children, long gone from the nest, with good educations paid for by her years in nursing.

Nancy, who spoke with the slightest trace of an Islands accent, was a stout woman like Dolly, but at five-nine or -ten, much taller. She told me that her relatives had recently immigrated to the United States from Africa and several islands in the Caribbean Sea. Like the other two, she boasted of her cultural heritage and sometimes spoke of the wisdom of a revered aunt or grandparent.

Nancy would become my right arm on the toughest cases on the unit, as well as my silent friend on the journey into the realm of the spirit world. She unflinchingly took on whatever chore we faced, and no matter how undesirable, Nancy performed the task with a sweetness and loving touch that always astounded me.

She seldom talked about her Caribbean heritage, but I came to sense that it had been distilled into her very being by the women in her family. She told me although she was a second-generation American, her mother, aunts, and grandmothers had made sure she did not lose her knowledge of the Islands' cultures. She never put a name on her family's traditional beliefs, but I knew they were rooted deeply in animism, because to Nancy every living thing clearly had a spirit of its own.

As a child, I had felt a powerful kinship with all things in Nature, and now Nancy was silently teaching me by example to look and listen more closely to every creature, no matter how insignificant. Whenever she heard a bird sing, her large black eyes would turn toward that sound as another person might respond to a voice calling out their name.

Once, when we were standing in the parking lot saying our good-byes for the day, a small wind came up and blew across our faces. As the breeze ruffled a strand of hair on her forehead, the huge woman smiled in recognition. I thought she was about to speak to the spirits in the wind.

She treated her demented patients the same way, with great dignity and respect, despite their often wretched conditions. Many times I listened as this large, gentle woman cooed pleasantly while washing and powdering an old patient's bottom in preparation for changing a soiled diaper. She never scolded a patient for making a mess in the bed or spilling food in the dining room. No matter how disrespectful the old person was to her, Nancy was undaunted and endlessly forgiving of even the most vile insult or violent action.

The patient population at the Plantation resembled a textbook of case studies in the common chronic diseases of aging. Their prognoses varied widely. For example, Randy R. was a seventy-three-year-old white male undergoing treatment for obsessive-compulsive disorder. His cognitive skills were intact, and a regime of antianxiety drugs held out promise that he would enjoy a complete recovery. Frank L. was almost ten years younger than Randy, but his disease, Huntington's, was progressive and irreversible. There was no prospect that his drug treatment program would do anything but postpone his physical and mental decline. He was already confined to a wheelchair, and two nurses were required to move him from his chair to the bed.

Some of the patients on the unit would have many good years ahead of them. Others would have only a short time. Some were fully aware of everything happening to them and going on around them. Others were in advanced stages of dementia, a condition that can be caused by more than forty different diseases.

It is important for me to interject here that dementia is not some dark condition that overtakes and blinds a person to the re-alities of an everyday world. Dementia, as I mentioned earlier, is a generic term for describing an acquired and sustained deterioration of memory and other intellectual functions in an alert person. It can be caused by a variety of disease processes. This loss of cognitive abilities interferes with a person's ability to perform many functions of daily living. Dementia occurs in both men and women and has no regard for ethnic or socioeconomic status. Its prevalence increases with age.

What impressed me from the beginning was how Dolly, Rose, and Nancy treated all the patients the same, whatever their state of awareness. Rather than dwelling on the unpleasant realities of the diseases, they focused their attention on the patient's "spiritual side." At that point, I was ignorant of any part of human development and aging that dealt with a spiritual nature. Imminent death was the only facet of these patients' lives I could see.

Still, as I reminded myself, I had already decided to stay on the job because, in the back of my mind, I knew I could leave anytime. As long as I stayed, I was determined to bring the best of my experiences and training in nursing to the challenge of helping these people. Perhaps because of my own family, whose members were so much older than those of most of my peers, I felt I needed to give this my best effort.

Dolly had worked in geriatrics for a dozen years and was undaunted by the seemingly hopeless condition of many of her patients. I watched as she went about her duties treating the demented old people in her charge as if they were individual rays of sunlight shining all around her. Her coworkers on the day shift were just as cheerful as she was about their responsibilities. I was impressed, and somewhat puzzled by it.

The subject of their respect for elders came up almost nonchalantly during the course of chitchat about the Cherokee Indian Reservation in North Carolina, where Dolly's family spent part of each year. That day—I believe it was during the preparation of the afternoon medications—my nursing assistant, Nancy, had joined us.

By this time I knew there was something very "different" about this trio of caregivers. It was something I could not quite put my finger on, and something more than just their exceptional rapport with their patients. It was like nothing I had ever witnessed before in my years in nursing.

When Nancy came in, she remarked on how rude a visiting relative had acted toward one of the patients.

"I wish that was a rare occurrence," I said, then went on to lament the way old people are scorned in our youth-oriented society.

"Not on the reservation," said Dolly. "Younger people revere the elders. Only the elders have lived long enough to have the knowledge that earns this respect."

"Ah, that's why you are so good with the old people," I said.

This comment led to further discussion about Native American customs and beliefs concerning the esteemed role of the aged in the tribe, particularly the spirits of the elderly. A demented elder was deemed to have extraspecial gifts. I listened with interest as each of the women described her ancestral beliefs. This respect for the elderly was common to all of them. But when it came to discussing things of the spirit world, Dolly was clearly in charge.

Because I was aware of the chronic shortages in geriatric nursing, I was not surprised to find that all of the front-line nurses were from different ethnic groups. I mention the ethnic origins and heritage of my three coworkers because their cultural background, training, and belief systems were soon to become as important to my education as the advanced science courses in my doctoral degree program.

While I knew that all three were well trained in Western medical technology, I soon learned they doggedly called on the rich shamanistic lore of their ancestors in dealing with these elderly patients. Their teaching was gradually to become an unofficial second major in my course of education, but at the time I was simply enchanted by their conduct with the patients.

Of course, our workload, looking after two dozen demented elders, assured there would be little chance to goof off. Somehow we did manage to get together on those rare occasions when the patients were all medicated, fed, clean, and mostly sleeping. Those special afternoon chats with Dolly, Rose, and Nancy about the spiritual nature of our patients became an important part of my days at the Plantation.

Slowly I was told of the little-known roles and responsibilities of the male and female shamans and seers in the tribes and clans. I was intrigued, and expressed a genuine and enthusiastic interest in learning more about their customs and beliefs, especially those having to do with spirits and shamanism.

Before long, Dolly and Rose were routinely pointing out one or another of the demented old people and saying "The spirits are active with that one today." They mentioned vibrant spirits they could see around seemingly mindless patients. One day Dolly made a simple statement that would ultimately alter my views on all of the diseases of aging—including Alzheimer's with its overwhelming consequence of dementia.

"The farther these diseases progress, the more spiritually active these people become," she said. "Deborah, remember that. Their spirits can always hear you, even if their brains don't appear to be working very well."

I saw nothing out of the ordinary, but I listened in silence, fascinated by the earnest way Dolly and the other two women assured me that there were spirits actively moving about the place. For a long time I suspected my new work companions might be pulling my leg. But if that was the case, they were doing a pretty credible job of making up their elaborate jokes.

My own basic nurse's training, advanced courses in medicine, and experiences in the real world of healthcare had been rooted in the pure sciences of Western medicine, with little or no room for the unseen. If it couldn't be measured in a test tube or cultured on a Petri dish, it simply didn't exist.

After my studies at St. Mary's Catholic Hospital Nursing School in Knoxville, I had gone to work in the Knoxville hospital where I had done some of my training. But I was restless for more education, and a college in Atlanta offered to credit some of my course work at the University of Tennessee toward a bachelor's degree.

Maybe, too, I was restless to leave the place where I had spent my whole life and to venture forth into the "real world."

All nursing education programs focused on the treatment of symptoms of the patients' diseases. Requests for spiritual counseling were directed to hospital chaplains, priests, or family ministers. My subsequent training for a degree focused on the biological under-pinnings of diseases, but again there was no room for the spirit in the realm of science. As I worked more and more with doctors, I was constantly reminded that my job was to care for and treat the *diseases* of the patients.

I had experienced only one supernatural or phenomenal event in my adult life, which I had deliberately avoided describing to anyone in my no-nonsense world of medicine. Somehow I felt it would be okay to tell these three women, though. At first I only hinted at the experience, not completely at ease. But Dolly and Rose encouraged me to elaborate. Finally I felt comfortable enough to share with them the unusual events I had witnessed—or sensed—during my uncle's funeral only a few years earlier. They didn't laugh and they didn't act incredulous. I breathed a sigh of relief when they told me that such happenings were not unusual among their peoples. For those who knew about the spirit world, they said, such things were commonplace.

My acknowledgment that I had a personal and powerful experience with the paranormal seemed to break down the last wall of suspicion between us.

As the weeks passed, and I continued to earn my coworkers' trust, another ritual emerged. This one centered around the work itself. While the nursing assistants were busy with the patients, Dolly, Rose, and I went into the medicine room, which was really

an enlarged closet, to begin preparing the daily medications. Each
nurse had a red metal cart with locking doors, similar to the me-
chanics carts sold at Sears, where all the medicines for our patients
were stored. It took about an hour, sometimes longer, depending
on the drug concoctions, to sort out all the prescribed pills and
potions. Medicine was dispensed three times on the day shift: at 9
A.M., noon, and 2 P.M. Most of the patients also received medication
at intervals throughout the two night shifts.

Because these medications were a major part of the patients'
treatment regimens, Dolly, Rose, and I spent considerable time
together in this little pharmacy closet. Each patient's medication
program, as prescribed by the doctor, was very exacting. Some of
the patients could not take their medication without having it
crushed up in fruit sauce or dissolved in juice and unobtrusively fed
to them. Others had to be coaxed by any means possible into swallowing their pills. Usually a little extra treat of soda or juice did
the trick.

It was in the medication room where our conversations about
the spirit life on the unit began in earnest.

At first, Dolly spoke in generalities, and for a long time she
would not offer any depth or detail. She studied me closely even
when dropping bits and pieces of knowledge. Her information was
superficial. I had learned as much or more in my informal research
into the paranormal after the experience at my uncle's funeral.

Over the course of our conversations in the first weeks, Rose
began to add her thoughts and observations about the spirit world.
Her experiences were somewhat different from Dolly's. In addition
to her Seminole Indian background, she was deeply rooted in a
spiritualist African American culture. Nancy, who rarely participated

in our conversations in the pharmacy closet, was more of an observer like myself. She was the most shy about speaking of spirits.

The three nurses brought different cultural experiences and perspectives to the discussions we had when we were all together. But these differences, far from being in conflict, seemed to strengthen their contention that a spirit world existed in parallel with the physical world.

They were all devoutly religious in their traditional Christian faiths and seemed quite comfortable that the two—Christianity and native spiritualism—were not only congruent but complementary.

In our chats over coffee and working around the unit, I soon learned that these women believed strongly that animals had souls or spirits, and that there were also spiritual aspects in trees, rivers, oceans, and even rocks.

Gradually, as they came to trust that my intentions were sincere, they spoke more freely. At no time did any one of them ever claim to be a shaman or to have any particular supernatural powers.

Rose always qualified her comments by reconciling them with her more traditional Western Protestant religious beliefs. From time to time Nancy conveyed information her Afro-Caribbean relatives had taught her. Dolly, unlike the other two, was more open about revealing that her knowledge came from the world of the Native American female shamans.

All three were secretive about their shaman beliefs, and as I gained their trust, they told me why.

"We are not trying to sneak around with our spirits," Dolly said. "But three hundred years of history among your people has taught us—and by 'us' I mean all Native peoples—that we had to keep our beliefs secret from outsiders."

With this said, she did agree to explain some of the basic elements of the Native American belief system. It is based on the
interconnectedness of all of life: human and animal, plant and mineral, earth and wind, fire and water, all interacting in a circular
pattern. Space and time are unnaturally imposed restrictions on that
pattern. Linear numerical time, as the Europeans calculate it, inter-
rupts the natural circular flow, because it imposes a finite beginning
and end. Such restrictions and interruptions limit one's life to a
single dimension, when in truth there are many dimensions.

"Deborah, as long as you live in the one-dimensional world
taught to you by your ancestors," Dolly cautioned, "you cannot
know anything except what you can discern with your physical
senses. From that point of view, these patients of ours will only be
what they physically appear to be—demented, old, and dying."

Dolly told me that even in North America, the Native people
had a much older basis for their knowledge than that which was
taught by traditional Western religions.

"The teachings of your people are only five thousand years old.
We have an oral history of *fifty* thousand years to support our systems of belief," she insisted. "Our people stopped trying to share it
with outsiders because most of them, like your ancestors, could
think only in the one dimension of their elders. So they rejected it.
Most still do."

Months passed before I could gain the women's complete confidence. We shared many, many small triumphs and failures with
our patients—one tiny heartbreak or little joy at a time—before I
was accepted as a full member of the talking circle that had formed
in the unit's tiny medicine room.

After a while, Dolly was apparently so impressed with my eagerness to learn about the spirit world that she spoke with the women elders of her tribe about me. When she came back from one of her frequent weekend trips to North Carolina, she told me the elders had sent me a gift. In her hands was an exquisite piece of tribal beadwork.

"It was beaded especially for you," she said, handing me a colorful barrette for my hair. "The black beaded thunderbird in the center and the green and orange beads that form the background were chosen just for you. They hold a special meaning to the members of my tribe. The Thunderbird is a sacred symbol to my people. It is the conveyor of aspiration to enlightened action."

Dolly spoke in a solemn tone.

"The grandmothers have listened to the things I tell them about you. They have given me permission to guide you," she said. "Slowly, of course. You are not ready for too much knowledge at this point."

"Your grandmothers?" I asked. "Are these the women who sent me the gift?"

"All of the old women on the reservation are our grandmothers," Dolly said. "They are the keepers of the knowledge about the spirit world. They see that your heart is sincere. But they want me to tell you that you must learn to listen to the messages of your own spirit first, before you can begin to hear messages from other spirits."

"Are these grandmothers the shamans you talk about?" I asked.

"Some might call them that," Dolly answered. "We just call them grandmothers, in your language. A shaman, to us, is a person who journeys into the sacred world and shares with people the visions brought back from that world—often through music, dance, or simple storytelling. This sharing can also take the form of art, like sand paintings or the Aboriginal dot paintings. A shaman may be male or female, and any age in human terms. Whether a person is a so-called shaman depends more on the stage of spiritual development than on years in this life. A shaman is ageless."

In all of our conversations about shamans, I was never given any real insight into their mystical calling to duty or to their rituals. Some secrets are just too sacred to the Native American people to be discussed, especially with a Westerner. I was able to glean from small bits and pieces of conversations that there was a different role for the male and female with special gifts and powers. It became clear to me that the female shaman was often viewed as a person who played a more passive role, almost as a communicator with the spirit world rather than a conjurer or manipulator of spirits. Dolly once told me this was an inaccurate image of female shamans but did not elaborate. My three friends seemed content just to recognize and acknowledge the beings from the spirit world that they encountered as they went about their earthly chores.

Rose, who was particularly religious and spoke of attending Sunday worship services in her Afro-Protestant congregation with her husband on a regular basis, often said that women had to take a leadership role in church to make sure the menfolk stayed involved. But she acknowledged that in her faith the male churchmen were the leaders.

My nurse's aide, Nancy, was raised Baptist after her family immigrated to the States, but she clung tenaciously to her Caribbean heritage. She said the older women in her family had exposed her to Santería teachings. Almost sheepishly she added that she had also been exposed to numerous voodoo rituals. She was comfortable with having been raised a Baptist, and when she was in circles with Baptists, she was okay. However, she admitted that she had also been considered a little kooky by her friends when she was a girl, because she openly acknowledged her beliefs in the whole Caribbean spiritualist dimension of dual existence and the animist nature in all living things. She knew all about the hex, herb power, potions, and the rites and rituals of the Caribbean and Latin American cultures. I had the feeling she was afraid to speak too much about her spiritual beliefs because she had been tormented over Santería and perhaps even voodoo rituals practiced by her family in childhood.

My nurse friends never evoked or called up spirits. They never seemed to seek special favors from the spirit world or ask the spirits they observed to do anything special other than whatever it was the spirits seemed to be doing at the time. When they did react to whatever they saw in the spiritual dimension, it was in the form of almost prayerful reverence, and then they uniformly spoke with respect and awe to "the Creator." With my Western upbringing, this concept of a single deity was not difficult to accept or understand. This Creator was not unlike every man's God, no matter what name is used.

As I turned the little gift Dolly had brought me from the elders over in my hand, it seemed to radiate heat. I was so deeply moved by the grandmothers' gift that tears welled up in my eyes. I understood this was their way of expressing to me a modest level of their trust.

During my free time away from work, I began reading more about the cultures of indigenous groups around the world. Whenever I was in the library selecting books for my graduate degree course work, I also threw in a book or two on cross-cultural studies. Almost everything I read, particularly the more recent literature on shamanism, dealt with a spiritual dimension of the human being that Western science hardly acknowledges or, in most cases, outright debunks.

Several times I asked Dolly point-blank, "Are you a shaman?"

She looked at me with a twinkle in her eye and laughed. If I pressed her for an answer, she would usually walk away.

Each time I tried to pin her down with a really difficult question, or drill down into the meaning of something she had shared with me about the spirit world beyond our senses, Dolly demurred.

"Deborah, your head and your heart are disconnected. You cannot understand the answers to that question right now."

If I protested too much, she cut me off, like a strict schoolmarm dismissing a child who pestered for information before she was old enough to understand.

"You're a typical left-brain, linear European thinker," Dolly said in a pleasant, almost teasing way. "You Europeans can deal with life only in a one-dimensional, analytic way. Everything must be subjected to scientific scrutiny before you can believe that it truly exists."

I argued that she, too, had been educated in medical science, with a nursing degree, and obviously was very proficient at practicing Western medicine on our patients.

She acknowledged that modern medicine was wonderful but quickly added, "As far as it goes. There is much, much more."

"Okay, you keep telling me that I need to get my head and heart connected," I said. "How do I do that? What are the steps I need to take?" I demanded specific, structured steps. It was the pragmatic way I was trained, the way I had been educated to approach unknowns in this universe.

Dolly laughed at my impatience and answered, "Those are linear questions searching for circular answers. In other words, girlfriend, you are trying to put the proverbial square pegs into round holes."

Spirit Music

I KEPT MY questions to myself in the days that followed, as I tried to glean answers from just watching my fellow nurses at work.

One afternoon, as I was walking down the hall to give my next patient a bath, I heard Dolly's animated voice coming from one of the private rooms. She was preparing to give a meal to Mrs. Davis, a seventy-two-year-old widow suffering all the signs of advanced Alzheimer's disease. Mrs. Davis seemed completely confused and oblivious to anything in her surroundings. Dolly still chattered away, as she busily worked around the old woman. Although her patient did not respond, even with a facial expression, Dolly carried on as if the two were involved in an interesting and provocative exchange of ideas.

I stopped outside the room in wonderment. Dolly sat down to feed Mrs. Davis, but she approached this often complicated chore with a zeal that I would have expected to be reserved for the more cognitively intact patients. She talked directly to the old woman as she patiently spooned the food into her mouth. Even though she could expect no response, Dolly spoke with a cadence that suggested the two were involved in some deep conversation. I had the feeling she wasn't talking *at* her but *with* her.

I had seen her use a similar approach when she was bathing a patient or trying to get a difficult dose of medicine down one of them.

Mrs. Davis did not utter a word or give a single sign that she was even in the presence of another human being. I had watched the one-sided exchange attentively and was sure there had been no response or recognition from the patient.

I caught up with Dolly as she left the room.

"You look like you were having an interesting conversation with Mrs. Davis," I said. "What did she have to say for herself?"

"Oh, nothing much." Dolly grinned, as if she had a secret.

"How am I ever going to grasp anything in the spirit world if I can't get direct answers to my questions?" I demanded.

"Deborah, if you want to begin understanding what is going on around here, you have to start listening to what is coming from inside of you. You're ignoring valuable information your heart is trying to give you," she said. "Somewhere along the way, you learned to distrust that information. That's one of the problems that comes with living in a one-dimensional world!"

"What do you mean?" I asked.

"Have you ever had a hunch about something that paid off?" Dolly asked.

"Yes."

"Did anyone ever tell you to 'listen to what your gut is telling you'?"

"Yes."

"That's your spirit talking to you in both cases," Dolly replied. "Deborah, you have to learn how to listen to your own spirit and trust what it says, if you want to move about in the spirit world." She walked away, leaving me to ponder the meaning of this short but important lesson.

The next afternoon, when Dolly, Rose, Nancy, and I had an occasion to be in the medication room at the same time, I confronted them with a series of questions I thought would give me more useful information.

"I've heard you talking to patients who are all but vegetative. Why do you do that? What difference does it make?" I asked. "You might as well be talking to the walls. They can't hear a word you're saying."

My challenge met with unanimous protest.

"Even if they don't show it, their spirits are listening," Rose said. "I thought we told you that several weeks ago."

"You did. But *I've* never heard them," I pointed out, "and I've never seen them answer you. Like Mrs. Davis yesterday—there was no sign she even knew that Dolly was speaking to her."

"That's what I meant about your head being blocked from your heart," Dolly said. "You don't have the ability to listen to the voices of the spirits. You can't even hear the voice of your *own* spirit. What do you expect?"

After several more linear questions that yielded another round of circular responses, I finally had to concede that even though I was not able to hear a spirit conversation between these nurses and their demented elderly charges, that did not necessarily mean it wasn't happening.

A couple of weeks after conceding that they could hear spirit conversations I could not, I noticed Dolly and Rose had started talking more openly about spirits. As we prepared our morning medication trays, they seemed to be picking up where they had left off earlier.

"Our ability to communicate on another level has been nurtured by the tribal elders and passed on from generation to generation," Dolly said. "Many generations ago, before people moved away from Nature and into their boxes in the cities, all humans were in tune with the other side. Almost everyone was able to connect with the spirit world, just as many of our Native American brothers and sisters still can today."

Even now, she maintained, there are vestiges of extrasensory or perceptive abilities in most people.

"There's a little bit of it left in everybody," she said. "Think about it. You can enter a room and perceive that something's going on. Your gut is telling you to pay attention. If people have been talking about you or saying something they don't want you to know, you can feel it, even though you haven't heard a word. That's a rudimentary level of extrasensory perception. People acknowledge that ability and accept it."

"Not to mention women's intuition," said Rose.

"Exactly," Dolly said enthusiastically. She wasn't about to give up the floor, so she continued with another example.

"Before children are shamed out of it, they can see and hear things that adults refuse to see and hear. It's common for very young children to have invisible playmates. But when a mother hears her daughter talking to the walls as she plays happily in her room alone, she thinks, 'That's cute. No need to worry though, little Mary will outgrow it.' Chances are pretty good that little Mary is actively engaged in conversation with something in the spirit world."

"Really?" I asked.

"It's trained out of modern Westerners at an early age," Dolly lamented, shaking her head. "Is any of this beginning to sound familiar to you, Deborah?"

I nodded as I remembered my own childhood ability to "see into the hearts of others," and I could hear my mother warning me: "Don't talk about that kind of stuff. People will think you're crazy and lock you away."

"These old people are at the other end of the life cycle," Dolly said. "The child is being introduced to this new world, and the old person is preparing to leave it and go on to the next one."

Rose and Nancy nodded their approval.

"The spirits of the old people are nearing a peak of maturity as they prepare to go on to the next world," Dolly said. "The spirit world is especially active around patients like the ones we have here—elderly and demented, especially those who are about to end their journey with us in this life. They are not as resistant as young people or other old people with busy minds."

"You mean the spirits of these Alzheimer's patients are more active, even when they appear to be brain-dead?" I asked. "Isn't that just a rationalization to make working with these old people more bearable?"

"Girlfriend, it's all in how one chooses to look at things. From your unidimensional, linear view of the world, these old people are one step away from a grave. From ours, their bodies are crippled by diseases, but their spirits are not. Their spirits aren't even touched by the diseases. They are continuing to grow—no matter what happens to the physical bodies. We see and hear their spirits every day."

Despite my continued skepticism, Dolly told me that she felt I might have the capacity to look into this spiritual dimension of life, if only I allowed myself to be open to the possibilities. During one of our medicine-room conversations, I admitted I would like to believe what they were saying, but I was just too pragmatic.

"I believe we have a way to help you move beyond some of this uncertainty that keeps you from progressing," Dolly said. "Ladies, make sure you and your patients have some free time after lunch tomorrow. There's something I want all of you to see. In the meantime, Deborah, there's a new patient who needs to be admitted. Will you please take care of that for me? Her name is Cicely W. She's a hundred two years old and sharp as a tack. Her great-granddaughter is in the room with her."

Intrigued at meeting anyone over one hundred years old, I grabbed the paperwork and headed for Cicely's room. Inside, I found a petite African American woman with white hair tied in a knot on top of her head. She was sitting on the side of the bed, unpacking a small yellow valise and talking to the young woman moving about the room. She had one of the most elegant faces I had ever seen. Her chocolate eyes sparkled when she talked. The younger woman was her great-granddaughter, Lizza. They both looked toward me when I entered the room.

After the initial introductions, we all sat down so I could begin collecting the pertinent information about the old woman and the reasons for this admission.

Cicely W. was born and raised on a large farm in central South

Carolina. Throughout her life she had remained on that farm with her husband and their ten children. After all of her children had left and her husband had died, Cicely continued to live alone and work the farm she had always called home.

"I was out planting my spring garden when Lizza here came and got me and brought me to this place," Cicely said. She sounded puzzled. "I don't know why she did that. There ain't a thing wrong with me. I'm fit as a fiddle."

Her eyes sparkled with joy at she recounted the things she was able to do that were remarkable for a woman her age.

Her great-granddaughter spoke to her with affection. "Momma Sissy, we just want the doctors here to give you a checkup," Lizza said. "The family is concerned about you living out there on that farm by yourself. You could get sick or hurt, and there wouldn't be anybody there to help you. Your children and grandchildren and great-grandchildren think it might be better if you lived closer to some of us. That's why we brought you over here. We want the doctors and nurses to help us figure out the best thing to do."

"Shoot, Baby Girl," Cicely replied, "you get me checked out if you want. Then take me back home. I've got seeds to plant, chickens to feed, and cows to milk. I don't have time for any more nonsense after that. Girl, you know I've got a farm to tend to. Let this woman get on with her questions, so I can hurry up and get out of here. I've got to get on back home before the rabbits get in my garden."

Once the admission process was completed and Sissy, as she liked to be called, was settled into her room, Lizza and I returned to the nurse's station to talk. She elaborated on the reasons for the admission that she had given in the old woman's presence.

"She is a hundred two years old and insists on living alone on the farm. She's becoming more and more forgetful. We're afraid that either she will forget there's something cooking on the stove and burn the house down, or wander off somewhere and get hurt. In any case, the whole family thinks she needs to be living in a place where there are people to look after her. She won't like it, but we think it's time to move her anyway."

The anguish in Lizza's face was evident. She loved the old woman dearly and wanted only the best for her great-grandmother. She knew taking Momma Sissy away from the land that had always been her home would be devastating. She was looking for support from us and reinforcement that this action had truly been necessary. I tried to reassure her that her great-grandmother would be fine after a short time. I warned her that she might notice a modest level of confusion in the old woman for the first few days. This was normal and would pass. A single tear rolled down her face as she turned to leave.

Momma Sissy did not let the dust settle under her feet once her Baby Girl had gone. She was in the day area introducing herself to the staff and any patient who could or would respond to her voice.

The next morning I found Sissy sitting in the day area talking to a small group of people who had gathered around her. In the assemblage I could see a couple of nursing assistants and a few of the more coherent patients. I, too, was enchanted by this diminutive bundle of energy with eyes that seem to light up a room every time she uttered a word. After checking in with Dolly, I joined the gathering of people sitting quietly around Sissy. I wanted to see why they appeared to be so mesmerized.

Sissy was recounting her life history. Her parents had been slaves before the Civil War. After the war ended, they were given one hundred acres of the original plantation land they had worked, free and clear. Sissy and all of her siblings were born on that same land. As the eldest, she was given the farm when her parents died. Like her parents, she gave birth to her ten children on that farm. Unlike earlier times, each one of her children had left for work in the city when they were grown. Once her husband passed away, Sissy was left with no one—not even a hired handyman—to help her farm the land she had always known.

Like other members of the group, I became enthralled with her melodic storytelling. I sat in complete awe of this living piece of American history, whose life coincided with the span of the twentieth century. Fueled by the attention of the "young people" sitting around her, Sissy recited some of the monumental events she had witnessed: boys going off to fight in both world wars, the first automobiles, airplanes, indoor plumbing and electricity, women going to work in the plants during the war, the Great Depression, television, moving picture shows, and three generations of children growing to adulthood. She prided herself on staying current. She thanked her ten children, twenty-three grandchildren, and seven great-grandchildren for helping her "to keep up with things goin' on."

Sissy continued to tell her stories while Dolly, Rose, and I went about our morning duties.

"Make sure the patients who are ambulatory or capable of sitting up get to the day area at one o'clock," Dolly said. "I have a surprise for everyone."

At the appointed hour, every patient who could walk or be

wheeled to the designated location was present and ready for the promised surprise. In the center of the activity room sat a TV monitor and VCR. The group chatter sounded like a classroom of restless children waiting for the recess bell to ring so they could go outside to play. When Dolly moved to the front of the group, everyone grew quiet.

"Ladies and gentlemen, last night there was a special documentary program on the public television station I thought you might enjoy. I made a tape recording of it so that you could watch it this afternoon. The program is called *Amazing Grace*. It was filmed in various community centers and country churches across the South. You will hear different groups of people singing their version of 'Amazing Grace.' Then people will talk about what the song means to them."

As the video began to play, strains of the first rendition of "Amazing Grace" filled the unit. Patients who had refused to join the group earlier began to wander out of their rooms, as if drawn to the music.

For the next hour, Dolly, Rose, and I stood behind the counter at the nurse's station, watching the faces of our patients. Their eyes were glued to the television screen. They ranged in age from 62 to 102 years old. Most had some form of dementia. Many could barely comprehend what was happening around them. Others gave the appearance that they could actually hear the music and understand the words. They were tapping their feet, clapping their hands, and singing along with the music. Despite their various levels of awareness about what was happening, every patient began rocking back and forth to the rhythmic sounds filling the room. Dolly, Rose, and

I joined in with the group as they sang the words to another version of "Amazing Grace."

My eyes fixed on old Mrs. Davis, who had shown no response when Dolly was feeding her the day before—or at any time since she had been on the unit, for that matter. From her place on the sofa, she was moving her body slowly to the music. When the music stopped, she returned to her nonresponsive state until the next version began to play. Despite her curved spine from osteoarthritis, it seemed Mrs. Davis literally sat taller than before.

Others I had observed around the unit were responding too. A sixty-two-year old former cardiologist with Alzheimer's, who now recognized no one but his wife, was staring at the TV with a new smile locked on his face. A severely depressed and almost unresponsive Mrs. Richey lightly tapped her right foot to the songs. An old Polish immigrant, Mrs. Chichkov, whose Alzheimer's was worse to deal with because she spoke not a word of English, was watching the others react and followed their lead. When Momma Sissy began to clap, Mrs. Chichkov clapped too. An eighty-three-year-old woman, Mrs. Walker, who could neither speak nor move from the neck down due to severe injuries from an automobile accident, showed her pleasure at the music in the only way she could. Large tears rolled down her cheeks. I was sure they were tears of happiness.

"If I didn't know better, I could swear we were in some old country church," I said. "Look at Momma Sissy. From that smile and serene look on her face, I could believe she was listening to the voices of a choir of heavenly angels."

"That's why I brought it!" Dolly replied. "No matter how demented these old people get, they always respond to the music— especially when it is a tune that was popular in their time. Their spirits connect with the spirit of the music. It helps to calm them down when they hear something familiar. Sometimes it brings back memories of a better time in their lives. Look at these people." There was a chuckle in her voice. "Their spirits are dancing all over the place. Can you see them, Deborah?"

"No, I can't," I said. "But what you're saying makes sense to me. I've seen music touch the hearts of people when nothing else could."

"Finally we're making some headway," Dolly said with a sigh. "At least now we have identified one doorway into the spirit world that your linear mind can understand. We'll use that as a beginning."

Suddenly I felt a sense of relief. Here was a piece of the spirit world I could grasp. Music had always been a part of my life. I loved all types—classical, contemporary, country, gospel, regional, as well as music from other countries. Ironically, as much as I loved it, I had never thought of music as having a spirit of its own. I had always viewed it as a manifestation of the human spirit's attempt to express itself. According to Dolly, this idea was only partly true. It was another example of my one-dimensional thinking processes.

"Music has a spirit of its own," she told me. "It emits a form of energy that can touch anything that comes in contact with it— people, animals, and plants." She reminded me of some of the recent scientific studies that demonstrated a positive effect of classical music on plant growth. "If classical music can make plants grow, then why can't a song like 'Amazing Grace' perk up the spirits of these little old demented ladies and gentlemen?" she asked.

"It makes sense to me," I replied. "At least now *I* have something I can work with."

Two weeks passed without any further discussions on the spirits or the spiritual dimension that surrounded these old people. During that period, I spent a lot of my free time with Momma Sissy. She was always ready with a smile and a story about the old days and life on her South Carolina farm. In 1990 the population of centenarians in the United States was small. Being in the presence of one who was so vivacious and witty was a rare opportunity. I cherished the short time I had to spend with this treasure of history.

Momma Sissy's lively personality and unusually fit physical condition made placement in a nursing home near her great-granddaughter Lizza an easy and rapid process. Her transfer to the new quarters came much too quickly for me.

The day she was scheduled to leave, I walked into Momma Sissy's room and found her putting the last pieces of her clothing into her tiny valise, just like the first day she was admitted. Lizza was moving about the room, gathering up her great-grandmother's toiletries. I knew there would be farewells from other staff members and patients, so I said my good-byes to both women and gave Momma Sissy one final long hug.

As expected, Momma Sissy was showered with hugs and kisses by well-wishers as she made her way toward the door. With every step she smiled and thanked this one or that one for a kindness that had been extended to her during her stay. I was deeply moved by the manner in which this diminutive, elegant woman was making such a gracious exit.

My pleasure in watching Momma Sissy's grand departure was short-lived. There were medications to prepare and seven other patients who needed my attention. I returned to my duties and tried not to think about the loss I had just experienced. An empty feeling, though, seemed to overshadow the remainder of the day. The warmth and loving spirit that was Cicely was gone. She was beginning a new and different life in a nursing home, where she would see her family every week.

Years later I find some small bits of comfort and joy each time I recall one of my memories of Momma Sissy. Her spirit still has the power to warm my heart.

THREE

Facing an Old Enemy

DOLLY AND ROSE resumed their discussion of the spirit world a few days after Momma Sissy's discharge. My coworkers offered to guide me through other events on the unit that might provide me with a glimpse into another dimension of life. They cautioned that such exposure might greatly alter my present way of thinking. Spiritual crises could arise from time to time. My very core beliefs about life and death might be seriously challenged.

I had been intrigued enough by watching them work with patients on the unit to want to learn more, regardless of any threats to my belief system.

They warned me, though, that delving into the realm of the spirits would not be an easy process. There would be many roadblocks thrown in my path. Normal fears would be exploited. Some of the images that emerged could be frightening.

"From the stories you have told us about the multiple deaths in your family you have experienced, I suspect you have developed a fear of death that could become a major roadblock for you," Dolly warned. "Overcoming this fear will be important. Getting comfortable with death is the first rite of passage for every shaman."

I'm not interested in becoming a shaman, I thought to myself. *I just want to learn more about the spirit world all of these women keep talking about. Getting comfortable with this death business is another issue.*

During my years in nursing I had developed some very strong opinions on the subject of dying. Like most professionals in health-care, I had an aversion to the subject of death, with its additional stigma of being defined as the ultimate failure in the Western concepts of medicine.

It seemed now like a lifetime ago, on a foggy day in late summer, that I had left the pleasant isolation of my valley home in eastern Tennessee for the trauma rooms of big-city hospitals. But nothing in my early training as a young nurse could have prepared me for the years that followed. More stunning to my sensibilities than the strange new life in the city were the shocks awaiting me in nursing. Before long I would amass a lifetime's worth of front-line experience in battles against death. Any childhood notion I may still have held about a spiritual side to life despite my training in the classrooms of science and technology were scrubbed from my heart in the wards and operating rooms of modern medicine.

Two years after leaving Tennessee, I took a job in the operating room at a children's hospital in Atlanta. I stayed there four years, primarily because I loved working with children, and also because it provided me financial support while I continued my college education. One of the benefits of working at that hospital was that it paid for two courses per quarter toward my undergraduate degree. I worked at the hospital every day and went to classes three nights a week. I enjoyed the schoolwork and the academic environment, but unfortunately this was only a diversion from my day job in the operating room.

My most intense exposure to death and dying began in that operating room. The hospital was a major children's surgical referral center for the southeastern United States. We were the primary children's health center for Georgia, Alabama, Mississippi, and northern Florida. So we got the worst of the worst cases of critically ill and injured children from many miles around. Our pediatric open-heart program was one of three in the nation at that time. In the early 1970s, the only other places a child could have open-heart surgery were the Mayo Clinic in Minnesota and the Boston Children's Hospital.

My job on the operating team was "perioperative nurse," which meant I worked in the operating room, but not as a member of the unit performing the actual surgery. I was, more or less, the go-between for the nurses who worked in the children's wards and the nurses who scrubbed up and passed instruments to the surgeons. My duties included overseeing the preparation of the child for surgery and then physically taking him or her from the hospital ward to the operating room. In performing these functions, I literally had to take the child away from the parents, which was a very emotional experience for the parents, definitely for the child, and frequently for the nurse as well.

We were taught from the beginning that our total focus was our young patient. Our goal was to do everything to distract the child, allay fears, and make the operating-room experience as un-traumatic as possible. We had to stay with the child every second, because we became temporary, surrogate parents and the primary caregivers until the surgeon came to the table.

There were so many poignant experiences that I wish now I had kept a diary of the words I heard from children about their fears of going under for surgery and their questions about dying. Of course, no matter how serious the case, part of my job was to assure the children that everything was going to be just fine, that they would be eating ice cream and playing with their friends before they knew it. Unfortunately, that was not always the truth.

We worked with the anesthesiologist to put the child under, because in pediatric surgery very few procedures are done with local anesthesia. Then we stood by, ready to assist the surgical team, as needed.

I stayed with the child until he or she went under and then stood back, prepared to step up to the table and perform any task the surgeon wanted done, other than the actual operation. For example, if for any reason the child's body had to be moved or turned, I was there to assist. I didn't pass instruments like in the TV movies. I had graduated from that chore long before.

After the surgery, when the team had left the room, I was responsible for cleaning up and applying bandages to the unconscious patient. I transported the child either to the recovery room or upstairs to the ICU and frequently met with the families, depending on the case and the particular scenario.

I was often the first person from the team to encounter the anxious parents, allay their fears about the outcome of the operation, and explain to them what to expect next. I showed them what the bandages were about, why the tubes were necessary. I told them not to be surprised if their child woke up screaming. Sometimes I stayed beside them until their son or daughter woke up and sometimes, in less serious cases, I did not.

Frequently I was the front-line person to interface with the families at critical points during life-or-death crises. So I was on a first-name basis with the specter of death. To survive this tension day in and day out, like my peers I became an expert at suppressing the emotional upheaval which always followed the death of a child. It was my way of coping.

We had three small operating rooms and we were performing between nine and twenty surgeries a day. It was a modern hospital, and because of its affiliations and the surrounding federal and university medical facilities, we boasted of some of the best medical and surgical teams anywhere in the world.

We did not begin doing pediatric open-heart surgery until I had been there about two years. Then we started losing babies every week. We lost many kids, but we saved many more. When we lost a fight for life, it was because the child was so sick or filled with so many congenital anomalies that it was impossible to do anything. We did everything we could possibly do, but it was never going to be enough to save all the lives. Medicine could go only so far, then as now. But this fact is rarely an adequate explanation and never a comfort to parents who lose a baby. I was troubled by the part of my job that forced me to talk about death to a grieving young mother or father. Echoes of those conversations and the sound of their sobs gradually filled my waking hours and invaded my dreams.

Perhaps because we lived in this life-and-death environment, the pediatric operating-room team was an unusually close-knit group of people. When we were on the line, the surgeons, nurses, anesthesiologists, medical students, and residents were as one behind the masks. When a child died, the team lost the child. It wasn't the surgeon doing the procedure, or the anesthesiologist, or nurse; it was the team, and it was something we all felt. But in spite of the shared responsibility and the team support, my personal involvement began to take its toll on me.

Each death as it occurred, in my personal life or on the job, added to my growing fatigue. Even though my surgical team won more than we lost, I seemed to remember only the failures. Any mentally healthy physician or nurse must have successes too; otherwise no caregiver could last long in the intensity of the operating-room environment.

Certainly we had our impressive victories at the children's hospital. Our sustaining belief was that we were doing everything possible with the latest medicine to give these kids a chance at life, the best chance they could have anywhere on earth. We did some remarkable procedures. We successfully separated a set of Siamese twins. We performed pioneering work in craniofacial reconstructions that gave normal life to children with devastating deformities. For one such procedure, I was in the operating room for sixteen of the twenty-four hours it took to reconstruct a young girl's face.

Then one particular case came close to bringing me to the limits of my endurance—both as a nurse and as a human being. It is as vivid to me now as the day it changed my life more than twenty years ago.

A twelve-year-old girl was rushed to us for emergency treatment of a complication that had arisen after a recent heart surgery she had undergone at the Mayo Clinic. After returning home to Georgia, she had developed an infection from the surgery, a wound abscess in a part of the incision close to the heart. That's what we were going in to explore and treat.

There were two surgeons at the operating table, a technician for the instruments, an anesthesiologist, and the usual complement of support nurses and surgical residents.

The chief cardiac surgeon had taken the scissors to clip the sutures around the infected wound. The plan was to go in and, at the very least, clean out the wound around the heart to hasten the healing process.

As the surgeon reached down to cut a suture, the tissue underneath fell apart. We could not see it, but what also fell apart was the main artery, the aorta. The walls of the tissue surrounding the heart were so badly eroded from the infection that the aorta just exploded under the normal pressure of blood being pumped through it.

In an instant the smooth operating procedure became a nightmare. One moment I was looking at the child's face and the next into the horrified eyes of the team members circling the table. Their eyes widened, staring out from the space between their sterile masks and caps, as blood gushed from the little girl's body.

The team worked as quickly as possible, with skilled hands, trying to stop the bleeding, to clamp it off. But there was nothing to grab onto, nothing to repair. The infection had eaten away at the tissue, and everything around it fell apart.

When the surgeons realized there was nothing they could do, all activity stopped. No one moved. We stood by that little girl's body and watched the blood spurt out from her chest. Her heart muscle was still strong, and with each beat it spewed a geyser of blood three feet into the air. It continued until the volume decreased, and as the volume decreased the spout of blood slowly dropped until there was no blood left in her body. I watched in awe as the surgical team stood helpless.

When the heart stopped pumping, one of the surgeons said, "We'll close her up."

The assisting surgeon took a number-two nylon, which is almost the equivalent of a rope suture, and they sewed up her chest. No one spoke another word. They were devastated, but they said nothing. They sewed her up, they shut down the machines, they pulled off their gowns and gloves, and they turned and walked out of the room.

I was left alone with the pale little body because that, too, was part of my job—the part I hated most, even more than confronting the frightened parents of critically ill children. I had to take care of the child's body on the occasions when we failed.

What happened in that room changed me. Rarely can an operating-room outcome so paralyze a highly skilled surgical team and leave experienced professionals standing helpless and frozen. Their reaction alone made an indelible impression, but the incident had a more profound effect on me. It forced me to face a reality of my world that I had been avoiding. When I think of it now, all these years later, and after all I have seen in a lifetime of nursing, the memory still gives me chills.

I knew we had done everything possible. It would not have mattered if the little girl was at home or in the hospital. The surgical wound infection had eaten away at the tissue for days. The heart was ready to tear itself apart from the decay. The same thing could have happened as she slept peacefully in her bed at home, except with massive internal bleeding instead of the eruption we witnessed.

Our team had no medical way of knowing the tissue was so necrotic, so dead, that when her chest wound was opened up it would set off a geyser. And once the heart walls gave way, it was a very quick process, because she wasn't that big and she wasn't that old.

This is not an effort to alibi what the team did or did not do. No one else could have done more. But this knowledge did not make it any easier for me or the others on the team to deal with it.

I had worked with the child, talked to her parents, picked her up at her room, taken her in, put her on the table. She was grouchy, very irritable. That often happens with cardiac surgery patients; it happens with heart-attack patients as well. I was tired and I wanted to go home. Because of the potential seriousness of the girl's condition, the surgery had been ordered immediately upon her arrival. The procedure was scheduled for the end of the day, forcing me to stay over and miss one of my night classes. I didn't do anything out of the ordinary, but I did not welcome the little girl's grouchiness. And then when she bled out and my team left, I was alone with the young girl's body. Alone with my guilt for feeling put out over having my plans wrecked by another surgery at the end of an already long day.

I felt awed at the enormity of what had happened. One minute I had been tending a lively, grumpy little girl, and the next I was forced to watch her life fluids spurt out of her. And then I was left alone with her cold, lifeless body.

Death had become real, before my eyes, in the most visible, tangible way.

I prepared the body for a viewing by her grieving parents in another part of the surgical suite and then for delivery to the hospital morgue. As I looked at the girl, now so still, I kept asking over and over: What happened to the life force? It cannot have just evaporated. It can't just be gone! I understood the anatomy and the physiology, but something else, something indescribable, something not found in the textbooks had also happened.

The children's hospital was connected to the main hospital by an underground tunnel. Since we didn't have our own morgue, if we lost a child, I had to take the body on a stretcher through this tunnel to the other facility. That was a lonely journey.

As I pushed the gurney with the little girl's body down the long tunnel to the morgue, I felt "Death" had become my intimate companion. Until then I had believed that I felt challenged, even thrilled by the fight against great odds to save lives in the operating room. I considered myself pretty tough, professionally hardened.

I had broken the cardinal rule of my vocation: *Don't get emotionally involved*—not with the families, not with the patients. Go in, take care of business, correct what disorders can be corrected, and forget the rest. Send the patients back to the people who are supposed to be looking after their day-to-day wellness and happiness. "We just patch 'em up, we don't take 'em to raise."

After that, death became a physical presence for me, and I realized this new and personal foe was not going to leave me alone.

Now my strange and wonderful new coworkers at the Plantation were asking me to once again reexamine my basic concepts of life and death.

Despite my reluctance to delve into the subject of death and dying, I sensed there was something very important to be learned from these women. I still cringed inwardly at the thought of deliberately putting myself in the path of painful reminders of my personal losses—the deaths of my mother, my father, my half sister, and numerous other relatives in such a brief period of time. And I didn't particularly want to open the old wounds that had been inflicted by my years of working with dying patients in hospitals. Nevertheless, I agreed to submit myself to the challenges that lay ahead.

The Unbroken Circle

THE GROWING REVELATION that there was some inexplicable link between my day-to-day reality and the dementia
patients I had regarded as mentally beyond reach excited me as
I went about my duties.

I felt somehow more personally involved with my patients as I
took care of their routine needs. One morning as I prepared to give
Mrs. Chichkov her medication mixed in applesauce, the chore was
unusually pleasant. I could not help but remember how she seemed
to have broken through the barriers of both language and her
Alzheimer's disease as her body swayed to the music of "Amazing
Grace." She was still as noncommunicative as ever, but I found
myself chatting away with her in a one-sided conversation. What
had seemed awkward for me only a short time before seemed so
natural now. She did not respond. And of course I spoke to her in
English, not Polish, her native language. But whether it was my
tone, my smile, or my attitude, I sensed that she enjoyed what I
was saying.

Something had penetrated that old veil of silence, and I was eager to learn how and why this had happened. Dolly's explanation had been reasonable, and I wanted to pursue this tiny breakthrough with my other seemingly mute patients.

I would not have long to explore my newfound information, because I was slated to depart on what was to become another important phase of my journey to understanding this new spiritual dimension.

As part of my graduate studies, I had elected to participate in a training program on death and dying, given by the world-renowned Dr. Elisabeth Kübler-Ross. Dr. Kübler-Ross is one of the foremost doctors in the field of thanatology, the study of death. Ironically, my decision to sign up for this program was made months before any discussions about shamanism or the spirit world ever took place with Dolly, Rose, and Nancy.

Before I left for the first of my four training sessions with Dr. Kübler-Ross and her team, Dolly informed me that when I returned, she thought I would be ready for a more structured approach to my learning process.

I did not know it then but the conversations that followed the experience with Cicely and the music room were typical of how Dolly, Rose, and Nancy would conduct my education into the spiritual dimension in the future. At each step along the journey into this new dimension of the spirits, they assigned me a case—usually one of my patients, like Cicely—as an object lesson. They did not necessarily tell me what I was looking for or what to expect. I was simply instructed to observe the designated patient more closely than usual as I went about my duties.

There was to be absolutely no spiritual intervention of any kind on my part; and I was, of course, to administer whatever care the patient's physician prescribed and my own training demanded. At no time during this experience at the Plantation did these nurses ever substitute any treatment for the prescribed medical regimen. All three of my coworkers fully believed in the power of modern medicine and the importance of administering the best treatment that current medical technology could offer.

Before the women ever singled out a patient for closer observation, we always discussed the individual's medical diagnosis and treatment. All of us were trained in traditional nursing programs, and we were first and foremost dedicated to operating in an environment of traditional medicine.

But during the process of carrying out the doctors' orders, Dolly and Rose encouraged me to look beyond the physical symptoms and to try to see something more happening around my patients. I wasn't sure what that might be.

I did come to accept that the women understood and perceived things beyond my purview. I was simply operating from my limited experiences within my unidimensional view of the world and what I was reading in books.

At the first Kübler-Ross workshop, the didactic portion of the training program provided me with a concrete and important piece of information to use in furthering my understanding of the spirit world.

The program consisted of a unique, four-part educational series of workshops on how to cope with death and dying. In the first weeklong session, called the "Life-Death-Transition Workshop" my

classmates and I were fortunate enough to receive personal instruction from Dr. Kübler-Ross herself, whose pioneering book *On Death
and Dying* had brought her international recognition. The book remains the bible of the world's hospice movement.

My graduate advisor had suggested the Kübler-Ross course for
me because of my special interest in studying the problems of long-
term patient care and rehabilitation.

I had looked forward to going away for a week to the session
in Arizona and leaving behind the disturbing questions about other
dimensions and shamanism. But if I thought the academic program
would give me a break from the strange things I was seeing and
learning at the Plantation, I was wrong. The extraordinary program
at Dr. Kübler-Ross's workshop only served to bolster my wonderment about the whole human end-of-life experience.

A small number of medical pioneers like Elisabeth Kübler-Ross
were daring to look beyond proven and provable science for new
answers about the last days of life. At the seminar I was exposed to
a cutting-edge, modern approach to medicine, which was, in many
ways, a startling confirmation of the Native American shamanic
notions in Dolly's informal teaching. I would return from the
Kübler-Ross workshop in Phoenix with a new perspective on my
responsibilities to the patients on the unit.

The workshop program was stunning and unlike anything I had
encountered in my years of formal medical training. The small-group
discussions that followed the structured educational sessions exposed
me to an entirely new view of the death-and-dying process.

For one intensive week, I was closely associated with professional men and women from medicine, business, and philanthropic
agencies who were not afraid to question the ironclad rules of sci-

ence and medicine. In fact, many of the participants were boldly challenging the accepted orthodoxy because of unexplainable things from their own experiences with dying patients, clients, friends, and relatives. Many members of my seminar class were veteran health workers with thousands of combined hours of experience gained in cancer hospices and other centers dedicated to assisting dying patients.

Most important for me, however, was the fact that by participating in the academically approved seminar, I had been exposed to physicians, nurses, hospice workers, grief consultants, and other professionals who were looking at nontraditional approaches to dealing with death and dying. It was as if I had been given some official stamp of approval to examine the alternatives.

The centerpiece of the workshop was Dr. Kübler-Ross's Four Quadrant Theory of Personality Development. Each of the four quadrants—the physical, the emotional, the intellectual, and the spiritual—addresses a different aspect of personality. Dr. Kübler-Ross taught that development accelerates in the spiritual quadrant as a person moves closer to death.

The fact that this noted physician espoused a similar theory of spiritual development in the fourth quadrant supported some of the contentions being made by my new nurse friends. Dolly and Rose insisted that they could see the spirits of patients with advanced dementia more clearly than those of other elderly patients with intact thinking and remembering abilities. Since these old people were closer to death, their spirit images were stronger. And since their earthly mental processes were suspended by their disease, their spirit natures were the only things functioning strongly within them.

The goal of applying the Kübler-Ross quadrant theoretical model is perhaps not as all-encompassing as the shaman teachings. The model was part of an instructional tool used by Dr. Kübler-Ross and her staff to teach people about how and when in life we learn to grieve a loss. Kübler-Ross's theory suggests that there are four basic stages in human development. The stages begin at different ages in a person's life and continue to develop and overlap until death. Since the quadrants are depicted in a circle—a circle divided into four parts—it also suggests a continuation of the life cycle beyond human existence into a spiritual dimension.

The *physical quadrant* begins at birth and includes the development of the human body as well as the five senses: sight, hearing, smell, taste, and touch. Human beings and all higher animals are born into the world with the basic tools for these, including the obvious: eyes for sight, ears for hearing, nose and tongue for smell and taste. The sense of touch or feeling is a bit more complicated but, likewise, is attributed to physical nerve networks. For example, nerve endings in the skin convey sensations of heat, cold, pressure, or pain.

Physical development also includes the functioning of internal organs, such as heart, stomach, and nerves, which govern such sensations as fatigue, hunger and thirst, and balance. In each instance, the features of the physical quadrant are well known to us and quantifiable by accepted medical testing procedures.

If it all ended right there, the explanation of life would be far less complicated, and we would be pretty much like all the other living creatures on Earth, from bugs to bison. If this was all there was to life, I could have labored happily in surgical nursing for the rest of my days, since modern medicine has become proficient at patching up the physical body and even replacing failing organs.

But at about the age of six months humans begin to develop another characteristic, represented by the emotional quadrant. Relationships are formed from a need to love and be loved. When these needs go unfulfilled, the person ceases to develop normally, resulting in feelings of rejection, abandonment, and betrayal. Development in this quadrant can be identified, if not exactly measured, by a person's behavior and ability to deal with other people.

At about the age of six (experts differ widely on when this phase begins in the young child), development begins in the *intellectual quadrant*. This is the period of time when there is a recognition of a "need to know" and when the child begins to exercise some logic. Obviously, if this phase of development is not fully realized, the person becomes what some refer to as "intellectually challenged," and human potential goes unmet. In this developmental quadrant intellect can be measured to some degree by standard testing systems, such as Intelligence Quotient (IQ) tests.

Spiritual development, represented by the *spiritual quadrant*, begins in adolescence, according to Dr. Kübler-Ross. Development continues throughout life in all quadrants. However, the spiritual aspect actually becomes more intense as a person ages. Of course, spiritual development is the most difficult area to measure quantitatively or define in any scientific sense. Thus, science and medicine largely choose to ignore this aspect of humanity. Failure to develop human spirituality can be observed in some people as confusion or an aura of emptiness and in others as a lost sense of purpose in life and a strong fear of death.

Like my three coworkers at the Plantation, Dr. Kübler-Ross taught that death was simply a transition process in which the soul or spirit moves from this world to the next. She stressed that a person's spiritual quadrant actually becomes more intense as the person ages. Such ideas coming from one of the world's most respected thanatologists helped to add a level of confidence to my growing belief in the existence of a spirit realm and an afterlife.

When I returned to work the following Monday, I shared with my coworkers Dr. Kübler-Ross's theories about life, death, and transitions into the next world. Dolly and Rose spoke of the parallels between her theories and those surrounding the Native Americans' use of the Medicine Wheel. They were simply different ways of explaining the cycle of birth, life, death, and rebirth.

"Both are circular, without the limitations of time or space," Dolly said. "A circle has no beginning and no end. Stages of development overlap and continue in a cycle of birth, life, death, and rebirth. The circle is never broken, no matter what happens in this earthly world. To my ancestors and those of my brothers and sisters in other tribes, the medicine wheel was, and still is, the metaphor for all existence."

As Dolly talked, I suddenly realized she was sharing information with me that was usually reserved for tribal members.

"Our medicine wheel is cut into four directions—north, east, south, west. Each direction has special attributes that serve as guideposts along the path of life. Our medicine wheel and Kübler-Ross's model of human development are both closely related to Mother Earth," she said.

"According to the teachings of my people, the human spirit is striving to grow from the moment it arrives here until the moment it prepares to leave and return to the spirit world. Along its journey in this world, the spirit is beset by all sorts of entities from the spirit world. These different spirits are vying for attention and opportunities to influence the direction the spirit will take. Roadblocks appear along the way to distract the spirit. Deborah, always remember that the spirit's journey through this physical life is an endlessly fluid process. Its presence on Mother Earth is only a phase the human spirit passes through. It may come and go through several human life-forms or reincarnations." Dolly was on a roll.

"The grandmothers tell us that human life experience is the time when the spirit is most challenged in its growth. As for our elderly patients here, the grandmothers say the spirit is strongest in the beginning of life and then again at the end of life. That's why our patients' spirits are more likely to be visible to those who are sensitive enough to recognize them. The older and weaker their physical bodies get, the stronger their spirits become. That's why," Dolly contended, "our unit here at the Plantation has so much spirit activity. Casual observers who come here see the vacant expressions on the faces of these elderly demented people and believe there is nothing going on with them. But they are so wrong!"

At an earlier time I might have protested some of the statements Dolly was making, since I had no evidence of spirits floating around the unit. But I was too enthralled with her recitation to argue.

"The medicine wheel has been used by my people for fifty thousand years. It is the circle of life to those among my people who still practice their tribe's ancient traditions. The center of the medicine wheel represents the divine source of energy that comes from the Creator. It is physically symbolized as the heart. The human heart is the balancing point of heaven and earth," Dolly said, speaking from some long-ago lesson.

"It houses the sacred fires of wisdom. For those fires to go to the person's head, they must pass through the throat. Deborah, what goes through your throat and out of your mouth goes out into the world. What returns to you becomes your reality. The reality is in your head. If you say these old demented people are vacant mindless individuals, that becomes your reality. Their value is then diminished. But if you can acknowledge the presence of their spirits over their waning physical bodies, your reality is expanded. And their value is enhanced."

Dolly went on to say, "If a person's own spirit has not developed or advanced to its proper level of fulfillment, then the heart cannot adequately assume its role in balancing the person's thinking. If doubts about the spirit world spill forth from your mouth, your ability to know the spirit world will remain blocked when the sounds come back to your brain. Whatever you say, you become. If your heart continues to fill your head with its fears, its anger, its hatred, these are the only things your brain can know. Such useless chatter will prevent you from forgiving yourself over some bad mistake or forgetting your hatred or anger over some supposed slight or grievance. Unless you can forgive yourself, accept who you are with all of your talents and flaws, your head cannot listen to your heart, and your spirit cannot continue its mission of growth and development for the next life, the other world."

I was mesmerized by Dolly's words and the rhythms of her soothing, chantlike teachings. Her circle of knowledge continued to spiral upward.

"The Cherokee elders, and especially the shaman leaders of my people, have for centuries depended on the medicine wheel to explain the forces of life," Dolly said. She added that Kübler-Ross's model of human development supported the contention she and her shaman peers had made many times before. They could see the spirits of patients with advanced forms of senile dementia more clearly than those of other patients.

"Since these old people are much closer to death, their spirit images are stronger," she explained. "In the Alzheimer's patients especially. They've had to live with their disease for so long, their spirits have had more time than most to experience an accelerated development. That's why their spirits are easier for us to see."

All of these conversations around theories and models about the cycle of life were very important for my personal growth and development. Over time, when Dolly, Rose, and Nancy talked about being able to sense things around our elderly patients, I wasn't as skeptical. I began to respect the possibility—the *probability*—that they had developed those extraordinary capabilities they claimed to have. While I did not understand, much less believe, many of their claims, I could certainly respect another person's belief, especially if the results benefited the patient.

Still, my scientific skepticism overwhelmed their best intentions. I wanted and needed more objective criteria before I could accept the concept of spirit entities that were visible in this life. They were asking me to ignore my practical nature. I wanted something more concrete that my linear mind could comprehend. Theoretical models and stories of ancient tribal practices were not enough.

If Dolly said it once, she would say it a hundred times more: "Girlfriend, you've got to stop looking at the world with blinders on. You've got to stop trying to analyze everything so that it fits into a neat little box in your head. You must allow yourself to step out of that little box that has become your whole world. You have to begin perceiving more of what is around you and be willing to open your heart to other possibilities. That's what we keep telling you, and that's what Kübler-Ross was telling you."

I was still perplexed by many of the things Dolly, Rose, and Nancy were telling me—even more about some of the things I was beginning to observe around the unit after I returned from that first death-and-dying workshop.

As I began to study patient charts and talk to family members, the demented elderly patients in our charge, especially those with Alzheimer's, became more than case numbers and diseases. They were real people, who often had enjoyed rich and rewarding lives. Some had done exceptional things. Reminiscing with family members about their loved ones became another part of my patient-care process.

Dolly said she was beginning to notice a difference in the way I was responding to the patients, a tone in my voice, an extra touch of the hand before I left the bedside.

She said there was hope that I would one day think with my heart.

"That's physically impossible," I said, laughing.

"Deborah, the heart is a thinking organ too—it has an intelligence that is just as powerful and strong as the brain," she contended. "To develop an ability to see or sense life at the same level the shaman does, a person's whole being must be connected. The energy of the spirit must be able to flow through the body from the heart to the head. For this to happen, an event or a sensory process that requires the use of all of the person's human senses, including the person's extrasensory receptors, must take place.

"Once the channel is clear, a person begins to pick up many more signals, more information about things going on around them, than someone who is only using the basic five senses," Dolly said. "In time, girlfriend, you will be able to pick up that type of information. As soon as you get your heart and head connected."

With that statement she chuckled and walked toward a patient's room.

This process of spoon-feeding me little bits of information during unscheduled meetings went on for weeks at a time, appropriately enough in the medication room, where we gathered undisturbed three times each day. During some of the conversations, I found myself eager to hear more than any of the women were willing to tell me. On other occasions, I did not want to hear any more at all, especially about anything that was not positive and upbeat.

Dolly could be heavy-handed at times, particularly if I seemed to be unable or unwilling to understand one of her mystical points. Rose stood by silently during those little arguments that would arise. Often she was more of a supportive figure than an active participant.

By now I had apparently become a central topic of conversation for Dolly and the "grandmothers" on her Cherokee reservation. Dolly frequently returned from weekends in North Carolina on the reservation, brimming with new information that the tribal elders had cleared for her to share with me.

If she became exasperated by my occasional reluctance to gobble it all up, Rose gave me a look as if to say "It's okay. Don't rush."

Gradually, as bits and pieces of what the women were teaching me began to make sense, I could comprehend the importance of looking at the totality of an issue rather than just what appeared most obvious on the surface. I felt elated. The tiniest emerging ability to recognize something new about a profoundly incapacitated patient became a thrilling victory.

I was simultaneously studying hard at night on my postgraduate course work. At times it seemed there was just too much information for me to grasp. I found myself getting my shamanic teachings and my death-and-dying training mixed up with my textbook knowledge of traditional psychological principles.

Rose sensed my frustration. Some days she would follow me into a room where I was working alone, shut the door, and warn, "Stay away from Dolly. She's wired about some things going on outside of work. They have nothing to do with you. Don't get confused."

Both Dolly and Rose warned me on more than one occasion to be careful how I handled information about the spiritual dimension. They repeatedly cautioned me to be wary about what I was willing to accept.

If I had any hope for a break in the efforts that were under way to make me more spiritually attuned, they were vanquished when I reported for my second Kübler-Ross training session. At this workshop, I would be forced to undergo a spiritual healing process to eliminate some emotional baggage which was blocking my head's ability to hear the messages coming from my heart. When I returned to work the following week, Dolly, Rose, and Nancy all went out of their way to mention the clarity they saw in my spirit. This clarity was about to facilitate one of the most incredible experiences of my life.

FIVE

Angel in Waiting

DOLLY, ROSE, AND Nancy greeted the arriving patient as if she were a member of their family returning home. She was a regular patient who was admitted to the Plantation from time to time for specialized medical care. Sara H. was a painfully frail eighty-nine-year-old who, once upon a time, had been a true southern belle from an aristocratic family. The family had seen grander days. Now Sara H. was suffering from an advanced stage of Alzheimer's. This admission to the unit, like others in her past, was to treat a recurring and life-threatening urinary tract infection.

Her daughter, who was a younger version of Sara H., accompanied her and stayed with us while the old woman was settled into a semiprivate room. Sara H. was luckier than most of our elderly patients, because she had someone with her who really cared about her. Her daughter clearly loved and doted on her, even as the Alzheimer's was exacting its terrible physical and mental toll on the old woman.

Dolly suggested I take this case. When I protested that I already had my allotted eight patients, she gave me a knowing smile and said, "It's important, Deborah. I think Sara H. can teach you some things."

The daughter, who had not overheard Dolly's comment, had no problem with my being assigned her mother's case. During the past five or six years, Sara H. had been coming and going to the Plantation and other hospitals in the city, and just about every nurse who specialized in geriatrics had been assigned to her at least once or twice. Dolly told me the nurses loved the genteel old woman and assured me I would not have trouble with the addition to my caseload.

Sara H.'s pale, porcelain-white skin was taut over her bones. I thought she resembled pictures of Holocaust victims I had seen. Although she weighed less than ninety pounds, an elegance and beauty still radiated from her aged face. Her crowning glory was her thick white hair, which her daughter regularly brushed and arranged attractively, changing the style almost every day.

After we had settled Sara H. comfortably in bed and started a medicinal drip, we left her to the loving grooming of her daughter.

Dolly whispered, "I think Sara can possibly provide you with a chance to *see* the spirit of a person who is waiting to cross over to the spirit world."

"Why do you think so?" I asked.

Dolly explained that each time Sara H. had been admitted, apparently breathing her last breath, the doctors pulled her back to life by curing whatever potentially fatal infection had attacked her frail body.

"She's ready to go on to the other side, but her doctors won't let her," Dolly confided.

"How do you know that?" I asked, incredulous. In her condition, the old woman probably could not have told anyone about her choices for at least the past several years.

Sara H.'s case was a classic picture of advanced Alzheimer's. She had lost all ability to perform even the most routine functions for herself. Her body had been atrophying for some time, despite all of the attention her devoted daughter and nursing-home caregivers had lavished on her. Clearly she had been kept immaculately clean and diligently provided with whatever regimen of vitamins and medications her doctors had prescribed. But Sara H.'s condition could not be stabilized for extended periods of time, and the physical decline could no longer be postponed. Even though she still had some good days along with the bad ones, it was obvious she was very near the end.

Her daughter, Marianne, was in her late fifties, almost six feet tall, and dressed conservatively in clothes that reminded me of the wealthy matrons in my hometown in the 1960s. Despite her mother's withered appearance, I could see the strong family genes handed down to the daughter. The stately, aristocratic Marianne was almost china-doll looking in her ageless appearance. She had a smooth peaches-and-cream complexion and not a hair out of place, although I knew caring for her mother had to be exhausting, leaving her little time for herself.

Marianne told me she was married and had a family—two children in their thirties. But in the days that followed, she alone came to see Sara. During her regular visits, Marianne rarely mentioned her children or husband. She was completely focused on her mother and spent all of her time at the Plantation visiting in Sara's room.

I frequently passed by the door to see Marianne carrying on a lively, one-sided conversation with her mother, as if nothing in the world were wrong.

Marianne brushed her mother's hair for hours and rubbed cream on her hands and arms. Sara H. seemed to recognize her daughter and at times appeared on the verge of joining in the conversations, but her whispered words soon drifted off.

She didn't recognize the nurses who had cared for her in the past but did seem to know they were there to help her. Her urinary tract infections caused her physical condition to deteriorate rapidly. When the infection spread throughout her body, she became confused and fretful. At times she was incoherent and mumbling.

As expected, Sara's condition improved after the doctors placed her on a powerful antibiotic drip.

On one of Sara's rare good days, she recognized me as a friendly face and tried to talk, but her voice was weak and her prattle had little or no relevance. Occasionally the old woman actually made an effort to share something that was humorous to her. If someone else said something funny, her mouth quivered with the trace of a smile. This was not something we expected to see from a patient with advanced Alzheimer's disease.

By this stage in her disease Sara should have been almost vegetative. She had lost almost all motor function and already had trouble even swallowing her food. Her intellect should have already declined to the point that she would have had difficulty identifying objects or, at least, would have had experienced impaired understanding of the meanings of words. And yet I was certain I caught a gleam of light in her eyes, as if she understood even the most abstract comments made by her daughter or me in her presence.

Sara's case was certainly not going by the book.

Often when Marianne was there, I stood in the room and talked with them. Marianne became my conduit for information about the dear old lady.

Sara had been a homemaker from an established southern family, which had enjoyed considerable social standing and wealth until the depression ruined them. But from what I gathered, Marianne was financially comfortable, having married into another old family with much of its fortune still intact. I think Sara had a second daughter, but she never came to see her mother.

Sara H. had remained socially active until shortly after she was diagnosed with Alzheimer's and forced to seek supportive living arrangements. Marianne's husband objected to bringing the aged woman into their home and had convinced her it would be better if her mother was placed in a good nursing home.

Now it was clear that Sara was near the end; medical intervention was all that was keeping her alive. She slept through the mornings. Even the slightest exertion, like having a bath or eating, completely exhausted her, and she would sleep some more. As frail as she was when she was admitted, I could see her almost disappear before my eyes as each day passed.

Sara had apparently been a very tall woman like her daughter, which made her thin condition even more noticeable. In addition to the Alzheimer's, she suffered from an advanced case of osteoarthritis. She could move only her head and arms. Her spine, hips, and legs were frozen into a near-fetal position. This made it extremely difficult for me to obtain the many specimens that were required to monitor and treat her urinary tract infection. When I moved any part of her lower body, her whole body turned. Her skin was stretched taut across her bones, and her entire skeletal structure was visible.

Marianne told me her mother had been in the same nursing home for years. But now the management was complaining that she needed more intensive care than they could provide. Marianne wished she could care for her mother at home, but had long ago faced the fact that she was simply not qualified, even if her husband had supported such a move.

Some days Sara's eyes glazed over or she hardly opened her eyes at all. At those times I could never tell if she was asleep or not. Each morning as I drove the winding, wooded road to the hospital, I wondered if Sara H. would still be alive when I reported for work. Then, suddenly, for no apparent reason, she would rally and come back into this world. That's a common phenomenon in people with advanced forms of the senile dementias like Alzheimer's. They appear to be at death's door, and we think they're not even going to make it through the shift. Then, without warning or any medical explanation, they rebound.

As I remember, Sara's treatment was primarily limited to fighting the urinary tract infection with antibiotics and building up her physical stamina through intravenous feedings. I don't recall the doctors prescribing any other forms of medication for her. At that time, 1990, the drugs that would eventually be used to treat Alzheimer's symptoms were still under investigation by the Food and Drug Administration. Consequently, our arsenal consisted of neuroleptics, antianxiety drugs, and hypnotics to manage the behavioral symptoms—such as agitation and insomnia—that arose. Of course, we also administered large doses of vitamins and bulk-producing dietary additives like Metamucil.

On this admission, Sara's condition was like a yo-yo, although she had more bad days than good. The doctors treated the urinary tract infection, and she got better. Then, when it was time for her to leave, she took a turn for the worse. On three or four occasions we thought she could be released the next day, only to see her relapse overnight.

Marianne pulled me by the elbow to the end of the bed one day and in a whisper of frustration asked me point-blank, "What can we do?" She was feeling the pain of her mother going through this process time and time again. It was a vicious cycle that seemed to be going nowhere. Still, Marianne made it clear she was willing to do whatever was necessary to keep her mother alive. It was difficult for me to tell her we were doing all that was medically possible.

Soon after this conversation with the daughter, I had an unusual, almost frightening experience.

That late afternoon was very quiet, with most of the patients on the unit napping in harmony to the rhythms of the summer dog days of this southern city. I looked in on Sara H. and she, too, appeared to be sleeping. Her room was dimly lit, with only the glow from the hot outside sun filtering around the edges of the tightly closed drapes that covered the small window in the corner of her room.

Sara H. had been very ill the night before. We had collected a urine specimen from her that morning and placed her on yet another antibiotic drip, because the urinary tract infection was beginning to flare up again. Her fever spiked to an alarming level. The doctors were talking about starting the treatment process all over, from the beginning. I looked at her worn, weary face and murmured, maybe aloud or perhaps to myself, "How much more can this dear old lady take?"

The room was in semidarkness. As I gazed at her face her features seemed to brighten. My involuntary instinct was to look toward the window to see if a shaft of light might have shone through a crack in the curtain—perhaps the summer sun coming out from behind a cloud. The external light had not changed.

Sara H. had not moved, her eyes had not opened. She actually looked dead. The sheets were pulled up to her neck. I could barely perceive a gentle rise and fall from her shallow breaths. The head of the bed was slightly raised to aid in her breathing.

I was about to turn to leave the room and call on my next patient when the strange glow around her face intensified. The light appeared to be rising from her face or from beneath the starched sheets around her neck. It slowly drifted, like a mist or wisps of smoke, lighter than the still air in the room. I was startled but mostly fascinated by what I was seeing. I squinted my eyes, trying to make the indistinct glow take some recognizable form. I had to identify the source. I became alarmed, and I was snatched back to reality long enough to make sure there was not some gaseous mishap occurring from a leaking oxygen tank or some other explainable source. There was no respirator or other vapor-making device in the room.

As I watched in awe, the misty essence became recognizable as a gauzy duplication of the old woman in the bed. It was uniformly whitish, almost the consistency of a water spray. The form's appearance was distinct enough, at least for my brain, to recognize pale features similar to those of Sara H.

My instinct was to run out into the hall to bring Dolly or Rose into the room. But I was transfixed. I looked from the misty form back to the face of the old woman, still deep asleep on the hospital pillow. I felt frightened but not threatened. It was like the fear mixed with thrill I had experienced as a child when I took my first ride on a carnival Ferris wheel.

Normally my training as a nurse would have had me moving rapidly to perform some procedure. But there was nothing in my textbooks or experiences to address such a situation. Besides, I did not sense that my patient was in any way threatened. It was just the opposite. I felt somehow reassured that Sara H. was more comfortable than I had seen her in days.

My mind fought for a logical explanation. I could not absolutely know that what I was seeing was Sara H., or that this vision was really emanating from her body. The image hovered above the bed. I struggled for a concept to define what I was seeing. All I could think of was, some years before, when I had painted oil pictures as a hobby. I remembered trying to create the right contrasts of subject and shadow by mixing light and dark colors. My literal mind fought to see this almost-mirroring image floating above Sara as a shadow of her body, cast in the dim light.

The human Sara, lying silently below the image, had snow-white hair and porcelain-white skin. She was lying in a bed with white sheets over and under her. White on white in the darkened room created few shadows.

The object hovering above this pale woman was even less vivid. It had just enough light and dark tone to form vague features with little depth. So there was very little dimensionality to the real woman or the vision. The images blended, and it was difficult to tell where one ended and the other began. But I slowly accepted that I was seeing some apparition of Sara—an opaque, misty, unexplainable version of the human form.

Earlier that morning I had given the old woman a bed bath. She seemed to recognize me, and sighed her weariness. With her eyes half open she looked up at me. Her eyes said she was tired of it all, that she had had enough and she was ready to die. She wanted this intervention to stop. She wanted to go home.

That urging, almost pleading message seemed to be repeated now, although I heard no audible sound or voice. My mind just sensed a message repeated over and over. "Please. Please. I want to go home. It's my time to go."

As quickly as I had seen or sensed whatever it was in the area around Sara H., it vanished or went back inside her.

The experience was not something I could tell her daughter. And it was certainly not something I was going to write in Sara's medical chart.

If I had been in any other nursing situation, I would have tried very, very hard to erase the experience from my mind entirely. I probably would have chalked it up to being overtired from my work-study marathons. But I could not deny that what I had experienced had been vividly real. I did all the spot-checking for reality, except pinching myself to see if I was awake. It was real, all right.

Thank heavens I had some understanding coworkers with whom I could share this! I went immediately to Dolly and recounted what I had seen. Sara had told me she wanted to go home. She wanted the medical treatments stopped. She wanted to go home and die in a place where she could be surrounded by her family. I told Dolly this troubling message had been reinforced by the apparition I had witnessed in the old woman's room.

At that point it had become primarily a clinical situation. Dolly and I talked about my options, what I could and could not do in talking to the daughter. Of course, it was not necessary to warn me against mentioning my afternoon experience to Marianne. I felt the most unusual joy in my heart for Sara and strongly believed her daughter would have shared that joy, if she had known what I saw. But my common sense told me that such an admission would be highly risky at best and unprofessional at worst.

I wanted to drop all my duties and describe this experience, the apparition, to Rose and Nancy immediately. But that was impossible. Other patients began clamoring for attention, and I knew Sara H.'s daughter would be coming back to the unit at any time. My strange experience had to wait until the end of the shift to be explored with my spiritually sympathetic coworkers.

Still, as I went about my duties the rest of the afternoon, my mind was spinning between reality and the "unreal" experience. On one hand, it was acceptable because of the conversations over the past several months with my fellow nurses, who frequently mentioned such phenomena almost as a part of their daily routine. On the other hand, the experience defied all I stood for and believed in. I had watched this women's decline, I had watched her laborious struggle just to breathe.

I thought that Sara must have kept fighting, at least up until this morning, because she wanted to tell someone to allow her to die in peace. Somehow I could understand why, although my training as a nurse rejected her choice. For that sick, frail, and failing old woman, merely to maintain life was a struggle that was wearing her out. The struggle also was taking a toll on her daughter, because Marianne loved her mother deeply and completely. So when Sara said she was ready to die, I could understand it. In my head it was acceptable.

As the afternoon wore on, the experience itself began to frighten me even more. I now felt that the apparition was the spirit of Sara—perhaps the thing that some people call a *soul*. People were not supposed to be able actually to see a person's soul; at least that was what I had been told as a child. But there was no mistaking that this was part of Sara—it was Sara's essence.

It also frightened me because it made me begin to question my own mental stability at that moment. But as quickly as that thought entered my mind, I forced myself to dismiss it. I had to try to keep focused on my patient's well-being.

Although what happened in Sara H.'s room must have taken only a few seconds, it was permanently fixed in my consciousness. Three years before, I had forced from my mind the unexplainable encounter with the paranormal events at my uncle's funeral. Now I was listening to a virtually mute old woman, reinforced by some ethereal vision, and fully understanding that she wanted all medical intervention stopped, she wanted to be left alone to pass on to another place. Suddenly that seemed okay.

Was I hallucinating? How could I be seeing these visions in broad daylight in this most modern of all medical facilities? Was this a figment of my imagination? Was some thing or some mechanism playing tricks on me? Could I really trust what I saw? Did I even want to believe the experience? If I accepted it was true, my life would become more complicated from this point forward.

The only previous experience similar to this one was at my Uncle Buddy's funeral, which seem like a lifetime ago. I had sensed his presence and the presence of others in my departed family. But I never allowed myself to believe what I had seen.

I realized now that I had heard or sensed the presence of my celestial family members with something other than my auditory system. I could not describe which of my senses had been called into play, and then, as now, it could only be described as an extraordinary sensory experience. It was not a deathbed experience. With my Uncle Buddy, we were at the graveside awaiting burial.

Leading up to that experience, like this one with Sara H., I had spent a lot of time in close proximity to my dying uncle. I rubbed his back and his withering, aching muscles. He had lung cancer that had spread to his bones. Before he died, the cancer had spread to his vocal chords, so he could only whisper the last real-life conversation I remember having with him. But at the cemetery, his voice had been clear and strong. When his voice came to me, followed by the sounds of other relatives thanking me for having him buried with the family, it was like being frozen in time for a moment.

Again with Sara, it was like being in suspended animation, being frozen in place. When it was over, I was aware of everything else happening around me—carts coming and going, phones ringing— and there I was standing in front of this withered old woman.

I was trying to form a sensory level of memory to put it into a perspective that could be examined. If I could examine it, I could explain it—to myself and later to Dolly and Rose and Nancy. But as soon as I thought of words to express it, I knew I was already translating the experience into something it was not.

I could find no sense of reality in that dimension. I had no language at my command to explain it, even though I know there was some level of communication going on. Clearly I would not have been allowed to see this apparition had there not been some purpose for both of us to come into contact at this level. There had to be a reason, some need for communication between this severely demented old woman and myself. I was being asked to do something. But what? Ever since my childhood, when I had been warned not to talk about such things, I had always had real trouble using words like "telepathic" or "extrasensory perception." At that time in my experience I had not yet been exposed to the term frequently used in the bereavement and complementary medicine circles: intuitive communication.

When our chores were done, Dolly and the others approached me, eager to hear details of what had happened in Sara's room. They wanted to know what had made me so overwrought. By the time I told them my story, I was all the way back to disbelief. I gave them as much of a description as I could, but I am sure my tone and words betrayed my skepticism. I could not believe the experience was real.

My shamanic friends had spent weeks and months urging me to learn to trust my intuition and the information that was coming to me, in whatever form it presented itself. If I did not, if I *could* not, then I wouldn't grow. My ability to make any further progress in understanding other aspects of the spiritual dimension would be limited.

"If you keep getting the message, but you don't trust it, you will block off the path and your ability to receive it," Dolly said.

It would take me many more sessions and many other similar events to fully understand why my coworkers, especially Dolly, found this intuitive or telepathic ability so natural. They had grown up in cultural contexts that supported and nourished this belief system—the shamanic acceptance of this sixth dimension, a sixth sense. Their cultures honored intuitive abilities. With that support came a whole educational process that nurtured such natural ability rather than teasing or threatening it out of existence.

In my situation, coming from a traditional European orientation, I had to unlearn what I had been taught in the past so I could understand these new lessons.

Nurses were taught by professors and reminded daily by doctors to develop and maintain an emotional distance from the patients. I heard more than once that this professional detachment "is the only way you can cope with and survive the demands that will be made on you."

During my graduate educational programs in the mid-1970s, Western medicine did begin to acknowledge that some psychological and social factors might play a role in the biological aspects of modern medicine, but certainly there was no mention of any spiritual aspect. Economic factors also began to impact medical practice, and under increasing pressures to keep costs down there certainly was no time or money for the delivery of any type of "spiritual" nurturing. Since geriatric patients were nearing the end of productive lives, this was especially true for them.

I was always taught to use every measure possible to save lives and to keep the patient alive. Since the earliest stages of the development of Western or European medicine, when physicians began to take over from medicine men, health workers have been trained to heal the body and leave any religious aspects of life to the clergy. Death is not considered a part of the life cycle but as the enemy of life. When death occurs, it means we have failed to preserve life.

It just so happened that at this time these Western medical concepts were being reinforced in the advanced-degree courses I was taking. Soon after I started work at the Plantation, I was taking classes in the biological bases of human behavior. The latest textbooks offered proof that even human behavior should be measured scientifically through biological underpinnings.

So while I was studying the advanced sciences of Western medicine in night school, I was being introduced, by my new coworkers, to a spiritual dimension of the patients whose lives I was assigned to save. The empirical evidence in the academic arena created a jolting conflict with the world of spirits I was coming to know.

No matter that I could not sort out everything in my own mind, the experience with Sara's apparition did embolden me to talk to her daughter late that afternoon. But I kept the conversation strictly professional and talked only about Sara H.'s quality of life.

Sara H. had told me in her faint spirit voice that she wanted to go home to die in peace with her family, not back to the nursing home where she would likely be alone.

In the hospital setting, I could not tell Marianne that her mother wanted to stop all the medical intervention. But diplomatically, and with as much tact as I could muster, I explained the medical options. A complete cure of her mother's medical maladies was not possible; only a postponement of the inevitable.

After a tearful hour, Marianne thanked me and went into the room to see her mother. She came out to announce that she would be taking her mother home, despite her husband's concerns. She had decided to tell the doctors to cancel any treatments that would prolong her mother's hospital stay. The next morning Marianne arrived on the unit with an ambulance crew to take Sara H. home with her.

Two weeks later Marianne called to tell us her mother had peacefully passed on at home, surrounded by her loving family.

Sara H.'s spirit manifestation had given me the courage to intervene in another way on her behalf, with information that would make her final wishes more clear to her loving daughter. I never discussed what I had seen with her daughter, but Marianne was wise enough and loving enough to heed this message.

I suppose I hounded my spirit-wise coworkers about the experience with Sara to the point of annoying them. It was a huge thing to me, but their reaction was matter-of-fact. "Okay, you saw her spirit. Good." What had been for me a major leap of faith was to them just the natural way.

All I got for my astounding breakthrough was a little pat on the back—no rockets, no fanfare. I still had my doubts about what had actually happened, and told Dolly so. I also suggested that the experience had left me questioning my own instincts. Maybe even my sanity.

SIX

The Pendulum Swings

WORK TOOK A less dramatic tone for the next several weeks. Patients came and went without incident. I completed my third Kübler-Ross grief therapy training workshop over a long four-day weekend. Everything seemed to be quieting down. Dolly, Rose, and Nancy went about their duties without a single mention of spirits or my encounter with Sara's apparition. It seemed to me they were letting all of my newly acquired knowledge and experiences settle into my system.

This downtime allowed for some much needed rest. Being on constant alert for possible lessons about the spirit world that surrounded my more severely demented elderly patients had left me drained. Working around those who were in earlier stages of Alzheimer's or other forms of senile dementia, which still allowed for normal day-to-day conversations, was less taxing.

One of those patients, Ruthie T., was an especially pleasurable assignment during that period. She was a petite, seventy-six-year old woman with Alzheimer's. Her symptoms suggested that she was progressing from an early, mild stage of the disease to a more moderate one. Prior to her admission to our unit, the good days she was experiencing outnumbered the rough ones. With the progression of her disease, the pendulum of her day-to-day level of clarity swung in a much wider arc. Her rough days were now equaling her good ones. A particularly lengthy episode of rough days and increased confusion prompted her admission to the Plantation.

Ruthie T. was brought to the hospital by her devoted and loving husband, George, and their only daughter, Rebecca. Their chief complaint centered around Ruthie's behavior. Her family reported that she "just wasn't herself," and she was sleeping around the clock. They could barely keep her awake for meals.

During the admission process, George T., a thin, distinguished-looking southern gentleman with salt-and-pepper gray hair, talked at length about his wife and his worries over her present condition. His voice quivered as he spoke of wanting the doctors to get Ruthie's physical condition stabilized as quickly as possible. He missed not having her by his side. He wanted to take her back home with him as soon as the doctors said she could go.

While I logged in Ruthie's personal belongings on one of the patient chart sheets, George spoke with tenderness in his voice about their forty-five-year marriage, their daughter and her children, and their long-standing involvement in the community and their church. He told me he and his wife had always been close. There wasn't anything he would not do for her. He was devoted to fulfilling her every wish. *His* only wish was to have her back with him as soon as possible.

Rebecca, in her conservative white blouse and plaid skirt, looked like she had just stepped from a frame of a 1950s movie. She stood patiently in a far corner of the room, listening to her father. When tears began to stream down George's face, it was obvious to everyone that he could no longer tolerate the thought of leaving his wife in her private room at the Plantation. Rebecca gently took her father's arm and escorted him off the unit.

Ruthie slept her way through the standard admission process that every patient who came onto our unit had to go through: blood and body fluid analysis, chest X-ray, CT scan, EEG, and a neurological examination. She would remain awake for short periods, usually for meals and medications only. The rest of the time she slept.

George came to visit his wife every day that Rebecca was available to bring him. Poor eyesight had forced him to stop driving long distances, and the Plantation was a twenty-minute drive through heavy traffic. Some days Ruthie woke up and talked with him for a few minutes. Other days he sat quietly in her room for hours just watching her sleep.

After being placed on a new series of medications for a week, Ruthie became more alert and active. She sat up in her bed, watched television, and talked to me about her family. It was hard to believe she was suffering from anything beyond the normal ravages of time.

The only clue that anything was wrong with Ruthie T. came when people asked her questions that were very convoluted and confusing. Resident physicians and medical students were noted for this type of questioning. Whenever she was asked a rather complicated question, a quizzical look would immediately appear on Ruthie's face.

I explained her confusion to the group of physicians each time they came for morning rounds.

"Gentlemen, your questions are too complex and abstract. Ruthie cannot understand you," I said. "Try to ask her questions that require 'yes' or 'no' answers. Those are easier for her to understand. And please be as direct and literal as you possibly can when you say anything to her."

Once the necessary translations were made, Ruthie would provide the doctors with any and all information they requested.

Serving as Ruthie's translator became part of my role during her stay. First it was the physicians on rounds who needed this service, then it was Ruthie's family.

Helping George and Rebecca adjust to the changes in communication patterns required by Ruthie's advancing disease process was more difficult. Getting family members to alter patterns that had been established over a lifetime together was challenging, but not impossible. Both individuals in this case were highly motivated to do everything they could to improve their ability to communicate with Ruthie.

For reasons I cannot explain, my name was the only one Ruthie could remember among all of the staff members on the unit. Since I was her primary caregiver five days a week, one might think such a thing was not so extraordinary. But it was, for a couple of reasons. Alzheimer's patients have great difficulty remembering the names of people who are not immediate family members. Ruthie didn't have a close family member with the name Deborah. And there were at least three nurses from other shifts who spent as much or more time with her. Yet it was my name she called out on every shift.

Every day Ruthie would waddle up to the nurse's station, calling out my name with each step.

"Deborah, Deborah. Come with me. Come with me," she said as she tugged on the sleeve of my uniform. "Come sit with me in my room."

Soon the other nurses on the unit, including Dolly and Rose, began to tease me about my "shadow." Wherever I went, they knew Ruthie would be close behind.

Because Ruthie's condition waxed and waned, her initial stay at the Plantation was unusually long. Just when it appeared that she was well enough to be discharged, her level of consciousness would begin to fluctuate. Lethargy became the norm. Keeping her awake for any length of time became virtually impossible.

During one of these extended periods of lethargy, I walked into Ruthie's room to find her in a near-comatose state. Frightened that she might be dying, I quickly summoned Dolly for help. She in turn summoned Ruthie's doctor, who came immediately to examine the old woman. He reported that he could find nothing wrong with her.

Ruthie had at least three or four of these comatose episodes during that stay. Each time the response was the same. I would become increasingly frightened that she was dying. Dolly would be urgently summoned. She, in turn, would summon Ruthie's doctor. He would examine her, proclaim her to be okay, and then leave with a puzzled look on his face. He was never able to figure out what was happening with her during those episodes. Ten years passed before I learned that Ruthie had been experiencing mild seizures, something exceedingly rare among Alzheimer's patients.

Given the progression of Ruthie's Alzheimer's disease and her fluctuating levels of consciousness, I was never quite sure how much she heard and understood. On her "good days," she picked up every word that anyone said. On "rough days" she missed everything. My solution for this predicament: Call her by name and speak to her as if every day were a good day. If she missed something along the way, she asked questions, and I filled in the gaps. We had developed a mutual respect that allowed this approach to work. We capitalized on the strengths of her good days and adapted to the weakness that accompanied her rough ones.

My activities with Ruthie T. and her family went uninterrupted by spirit lessons from Dolly, Rose, and Nancy. They seemed to be occupied with other matters. The unit's census was low, so they took the luxury of some extra free time to work on projects the head nurse had assigned to them. As the agency nurse, I was never pulled into unit projects. I was being paid to give direct patient care, nothing more. I liked that aspect of my job because it also meant that I did not get caught up in hospital politics, always a distraction in any unit setting.

My "free time" was usually spent with Ruthie. On those days when she could and would talk, I learned quite a bit about her life. She was unaware that she had Alzheimer's. She thought George and Rebecca had admitted her to the hospital because she was "a bit run-down." She had no memory of her comalike episodes. She loved her family, especially her daughter and grandchildren. She had no particular interest in going back to her church work or her garden-club activities. She enjoyed having me sit and talk with her.

As the weeks passed, her condition continued to fluctuate. Getting both her medical and neurological systems stabilized became increasingly demanding.

Late one afternoon Ruthie's condition deteriorated significantly. Her outlook was considered grave. The doctors were not sure she would last through the end of the week if her condition could not be improved.

Having nearly completed my Kübler-Ross death-and-dying training, I was more comfortable talking to dying patients. I had heard stories through the years about elderly patients at death's door who made miraculous recoveries for no apparent reason. Dolly, Rose, and Nancy had been telling me over and over that elderly people's spirits could hear another person talking to them.

I figured I had nothing to lose. I would go talk to Ruthie's spirit. If what I had been told was true, she might get better. If it was not, then I could at least be comfortable knowing I had tried.

I walked into Ruthie's private room and closed the door behind me. She was lying peacefully in her bed. Her silver hair glistened in the sunlight. The ruffles of her pale blue nightgown were moving up and down with her slow and shallow breathing. I sat on the edge of the bed.

"Ruthie, it's me, Deborah," I said quietly. "The doctors say you're pretty sick right now. I know you and I have talked about how tired you've been lately."

I felt my heart pounding in my throat. Every word coming out of my mouth was a struggle. "Ruthie, I just want to tell you that it's okay to cross over to the other side, if that's what you really want to do. I hear it's beautiful over there. Before you go, though, you need to make sure you've taken care of your business with George and Rebecca. They love you very much, and they're really going to miss you when you're gone. So, if there's anything they need to know, you had better tell them now while you still can."

When I finished, I looked down at Ruthie. She was still breathing. She looked like she was in a deep sleep. I did not know if she had heard a single word I said to her.

My heart was still pounding as I sat quietly at her beside. I had never done such a thing in my life. The very idea of talking to someone about crossing over into the afterlife! Who was I to think that I could do such a thing? *Someone who cares about this old woman* was the only answer that came to me.

Within forty-eight hours, Ruthie made a complete and unexplainable recovery. Even the doctors were amazed at how quickly her turnaround came. What made the difference? Was it their fine Western medical treatment, or was it a simple, quiet session in which an old woman's spirit was given permission to cross over into the afterlife? No one will ever know. That didn't matter.

What did matter was that within a few days, Ruthie's husband and daughter came to take her home. All three left the unit with smiles on their faces.

Six months later, Ruthie returned to the Plantation. She had been unable to sleep for several days in a row. As a result, she grew increasingly agitated. She constantly paced about the house and rummaged through drawers. George could not get her to eat or drink anything. Finally, when he and Rebecca could no longer manage her behaviors on their own, they agreed that she should return to our unit.

Medications to induce sleep were initiated soon after she was readmitted. Within three days, Ruthie's sleep cycle had returned to normal. Her agitation subsided and her pacing ceased. By this visit, her mental clarity had lessened. Most days she could not recognize anyone—not me, her husband, or her daughter. She simply stared blankly at the TV playing in her private room.

George's gaunt appearance suggested that his wife's condition was beginning to exact a price on his health as well. He looked as if he had lost weight and gone without sleep himself. When I questioned him about the events that led to this second admission, he confirmed that he had tried to stay with his wife throughout the entire sleepless three-day ordeal.

"Deborah, I was so afraid something would happen to her if I fell asleep," George said. Tears rolled down his cheeks. Total exhaustion overtook him. His Ruthie was safe. He was free to unwind for the first time in many days.

The reality of Ruthie's condition was beginning to set in. George finally acknowledged to himself and everyone involved that he could no longer take care of her at home by himself. Even though Rebecca and her family were willing to take both parents into their home, the demands of caring for Ruthie and two preschool children made such a move impractical. Ruthie T. would need placement in a long-term care facility.

The unit's social worker began the long and arduous process of locating a placement site for Ruthie. Finding a facility that could meet her needs and her husband's requirement that it be nearby would take time.

In the ensuing weeks, George and Rebecca came to visit Ruthie every day. Frequently Rebecca would drop her father off, so he could spend the entire day with her mother. On those occasions, I would find him sitting by Ruthie's bedside, holding her hand and talking to her about memories of days gone by.

Sometimes, when George was talking to her, I caught a gleam in Ruthie's eyes. Was she able to hear him? Could she understand his words? Did she actually remember the event he was describing? I like to think she did, at least on some days.

Weeks passed without any word on a facility that would take Ruthie. George would not budge from the position laid down when he first agreed to seek placement for his wife. If they were going to be separated at all, Ruthie had to be housed nearby. If that was not possible, he would take her home with him, and they would manage somehow.

George had been warned by the unit's social worker that finding a long-term care facility with an empty bed near his home would be next to impossible. But it happened. A nursing home operated by George and Ruthie's religious group finally had a vacancy. It was located within a few blocks of the house where the couple had lived for more than thirty years. Rebecca could take her father to see his wife every day. It was perfect.

The day for Ruthie's discharge came quickly. George and Rebecca arrived early that morning. As they packed Ruthie's clothes and prepared her for travel, I went in to say my final good-byes.

George had a huge grin on his face and a peacefulness about him I had never seen.

"Deborah, my Ruthie won't be far away from me. She will be able to live in a nice place where professionals can give her the proper care she needs. And I will still be able to see her every day," George said as he and Rebecca wheeled Ruthie toward the unit's double doors. "That's really all I want in life now—to be close to my Ruthie for as long as I can."

When Ruthie and her family left the unit that second time, my quiet reprieve from spirits and lessons on the spiritual domain came to an abrupt end.

SEVEN

Unrecognized Treasures

SOME DAYS I could walk on to the neuro-psych unit and feel the restlessness. By now the months I had spent tending to the unpredictable needs of my elderly patients had prepared me for such times.

But this day promised to be especially vexing, from the moment I walked through the doors to take the shift-change report from the night nurse. Dolly, arriving on my heels, immediately mentioned the strange vibes too. Had she not commented, I would have chalked it up to my own cloudy mood. I had spent a wakeful night, interrupted by periods of worry over work and school, and my experience with Sara's spirit that still haunted me. Perhaps my tiredness made me sense the heightened tension in the air.

We were still preparing the morning medicine trays when it started—either in one of the patient's rooms or farther down the corridor, in the day room. The patients were fretful. First one, then several started talking loudly from their rooms, until it was picked up by others, chattering across the unit in a chain reaction.

I knew the medical term for the phenomenon that was producing the rising noise level. It was called *echolalia*, a stereotypical babble or repetition of another patient's words or phrases. With our twenty-four patients in somewhat close proximity, one patient would begin making a "la-la" sound and before long, others would be parroting the same sounds up and down the halls.

Dolly put down the pill bottle she was dispensing from and stopped to listen.

"The spirits are active today," she said in that matter-of-fact way that seemed to imply some age-old knowledge.

"Nonsense," I said, "it's just the patients in the sitting room parroting the sounds they're hearing the others make. They're just spreading their joy across the unit." I regretted my peevishness before the utterance was out of my mouth.

"You'll see, girlfriend." She laughed. "Before this day is over, you will see."

I had already learned that Dolly and the others were usually right, but I attributed it partly to their long years of experience caring for the elderly demented. Yet I was also now willing to credit shamanism for some part of their extraordinary sensitivity to things going on around the patients.

As we finished preparing the medicine trays, the women talked about vibrations in the unit. Dolly noted that in the Cherokee tradition, a person's thoughts and actions create vibrations in the atmosphere. Just as the drumming rhythm is used by a shaman to conjure spirits, Dolly said the restless, repetitive sounds of our patients could set up vibrations that might produce similar results.

A short time after noon, the phone rang at the nurse's station. No one was immediately on hand and the instrument seemed to blare urgently, louder and louder, as Rose raced to answer it. On the line was the clerk in the admitting office notifying us that we had a patient coming in under emergency conditions.

Rose called out to Dolly with some of the details. "It's an old woman coming in by ambulance—she has a police escort," Rose said, her voice loud enough to carry throughout the unit.

"What's with the police escort?" Nancy had joined us at the nurse's station. "Did she kill someone?"

"Not yet," Rose said. "She barricaded herself in her apartment and threatened to kill the neighbor who went to check on her. When her family came, they called the law."

Dolly wasn't as interested in the details as in getting ready to receive the patient. She ordered Nancy to hurry over to room 124A, a semiprivate room, and get it ready.

Normally we did not receive our patients under emergency conditions, so this call set off all of the staff's internal warning bells. Everyone rushed around like a M.A.S.H. unit getting ready for incoming casualties.

"Don't forget to lay out the bed straps," Dolly instructed as Nancy dashed away. The extra instruction was not really necessary since Nancy, as a nursing assistant with years of geriatric experience, knew exactly what to expect with an unruly patient.

But we were soon to learn that no one among us, with all our combined years of varied nursing experiences, knew what was in store for us in this case. My own doubts about spirit manifestations were about to be erased too.

The first time I laid eyes on this woman who would become so important in my future, her ninety-pound body was thrashing about under three gurney straps. All I could see was a tiny head of faded auburn hair and the emaciated frame of a body kicking and surging against her constraints. A couple of muscular paramedics held firmly to the gurney as they pushed her through the unit doors. Two husky armed police officers followed a few paces behind. From the looks of the four men, I could tell they were glad to have their fighting little bundle inside our facility.

Rose and Nancy were stationed in the patient room waiting for her. Dolly was standing by to show the emergency team the way to room 124A.

The paramedics and policemen hesitated at the entrance to the unit, as if they planned to leave the fighting old hellion right there and let us take charge. A tall woman in a business suit appeared for a minute behind the gurney. She took a quick look at the woman writhing on it and turned to me for directions to the admitting office.

Dolly, seeing that the men surrounding the gurney had stopped at the entrance, didn't give them time to retreat. She was going to make sure she had the benefit of all the help she could get, authorized or not.

"Come on, boys," she barked with authority. "Bring the lady right this way. We've got a nice little room all cozy and ready just for her."

As Dolly passed me at the nurse's station, where I had been told to "hold the fort while we take care of this," she hissed, "She's possessed!"

Before I could respond, Dolly rushed off at a surprisingly agile clip for a woman of her size. The paramedics obediently followed her, one guiding, the other pushing, the gurney. The two big policemen flanked the thrashing passenger on the gurney. The uniform shirts of all four of the men, whites on the paramedics and blues on the officers, looked disheveled. They were gone from my view so fast I did not have time to inspect them more closely for damage, but I was pretty sure they had not reported for work that morning in such disarray. The entourage wheeled into room 124A and the door closed behind them.

Immediately I heard coming from the room the sounds of muffled voices, interspersed with thumps and bumps. Dolly's voice rose clearly above the men's, efficiently giving instructions.

At just about that time my attention was diverted when the tall woman I had seen earlier beside the gurney approached me, accompanied by the admissions clerk from upstairs. The woman was attractive, well groomed, and, I guessed, in her early forties. She could have been a business executive on lunch break except for her drawn look and worry lines creasing her face. She appeared to have been crying, and her makeup was slightly smeared.

"You have my aunt here, I believe," she said with almost a plea in her voice. The admissions clerk handed me a clipboard with the patient's clean new chart attached. I noticed a staff physician had already approved the admission and marveled at the efficiency. Usually the paperwork for an unscheduled admission would take more time, but I guessed this little episode had been going on for a good part of the morning before we received the patient.

I scanned the admitting data.

Admitting Diagnosis: Acute confusional state with active auditory and visual hallucinations; probable psychotic depression.

Provisional Diagnosis: Rule out: Senile Dementia, Alzheimer's type; CVA/stroke; metabolic imbalance; systemic infections such as pneumonia or UTI (urinary tract infection).

The information at the top of the chart was Mrs. Melissa T., female, Caucasian, DOB 4/18/02, age 88 years.

"Is your aunt's name Melissa T.?" I asked.

The well-dressed woman nodded.

"The other staff members are getting her settled into her room," I said, and quickly added, "Don't worry, she's in good hands."

The woman seemed relieved but on the verge of bursting into tears again.

Nothing on the admissions form seemed out of the ordinary for the patient population we handled, but as the noises continued to emanate from room 124A, I began to wonder. Melissa T.'s aging body chemistry was clearly out of order for some reason that would be determined soon enough. Her admitting physician had sent instructions for the patient to be heavily sedated with tranquilizers "if necessary," and anyone could see it would be.

The niece paced around the small space in front of the nurse's station while I filled out the paperwork. Moments later she came over and stopped in front of me, clearly needing to talk to someone.

"I can't imagine what happened to Aunt Mel," she began. "She was doing so well the last time we were with her, just a few weeks ago."

The niece wanted me to know that she and her husband really did care for her aunt, to assure me that her Aunt Mel was not just another "throwaway old person."

Melissa T. had been living on her own in an apartment for many years since her husband died. She had done very well by herself and shunned any suggestion that she needed assistance. A few friends came to see her occasionally, and there had always been parties, luncheons, and dinners with the family. She was surrounded by people until "fairly recently," when many of her friends began to die off.

"And I guess we have been pretty busy lately," the woman said in a small, self-accusatory voice. "But we did just have her over for dinner a week or so ago."

It turned out, as our conversation progressed, that the "week or so" had actually been about six weeks. The time between visits with elderly relatives seems to fly by for younger couples saddled with the responsibilities of two jobs, children, and social obligations of their own.

I could almost fill in the blanks from the stories I had pieced together in the months I had been on this geriatric unit.

Melissa T. had gradually found herself becoming more and more isolated. As she grew older, she was outliving her friends. Those who remained were too busy to join her in the activities that had brought her so much pleasure over the years. She spent more and more time alone. With each passing day she grew more depressed. Her spirit got weaker and weaker. Soon she didn't care whether she lived or died. She essentially stopped eating or drinking much on a regular schedule, until finally she would go days without a meal. I suspected that over time her body had become dehydrated and malnourished. Then she arrived at the point where she couldn't sleep.

I knew very well from my training that sleep deprivation, together with dehydration and malnutrition, could lead to a psychotic episode and hallucinations. Her brain would lose its ability to distinguish what was real from what was fantasy. To me, these were all medically predictable outcomes.

Dolly had explained that there was something else going on in these cases as well. When an old person's will is broken, the spirit becomes too weak to resist. That's when the dark spirits, which are out there in some part of the universe, see an opportunity to move in on a person. An old person who arrives at that fragile state, both physically and spiritually, is highly vulnerable to an invasion by these forces of darkness.

"They can move right in and take up residence in a frail, spiritually broken body," Dolly had told me.

My musings were interrupted by more noise and thumping coming from the room down the hall. I thought I heard the sound of a dog growling but put it out of my mind.

It was taking an awfully long time to get the old woman settled down. I looked at my watch. More than half an hour had passed, and not one of the nurses, paramedics, or police officers had exited the room.

The patient's niece was now explaining to me what had happened during the hours prior to Melissa being wheeled onto the unit.

"I received a call this morning from one of her neighbors," the woman said. "She told me she had not seen my aunt in several days and went by to check on her. She could hear her inside the apartment, but Aunt Mel wouldn't come to the door. My aunt screamed at her from inside—something like 'Leave me alone or I'll kill you!' "

In response to the call from the neighbor, the niece left work and rushed to the apartment. She, too, could hear noises, which she identified as her aunt's voice, making incoherent sounds inside the apartment. But there was no response to her knocks, no matter how loudly she beat or kicked at the door. So she called her husband, who in turn called the police.

The police arrived and, with the niece's permission, broke open the door. Inside they found Melissa's normally immaculate three-room apartment in shambles. All of the rooms were strewn with old papers and magazines, furniture was out of place, and clothing was thrown about. The kitchen and living room were piled with empty cans and days-old food scraps. At first they thought Melissa might have come upon a burglary in progress. But when they confronted her, the old woman did not recognize her niece. She was hallucinating, and when the officers approached her, she tried to bite and claw them.

The niece had wisely called Aunt Mel's doctor and set the wheels in motion to get an order of protective custody established and an emergency hospital admission authorized. Still, the tiny woman had to be handcuffed at one point so the arriving ambulance crew could get her strapped to a gurney for the trip to our facility.

Melissa T.'s niece looked at me for reassurance. "Will she be okay?" she asked. I said that we had seen this before—often—and told her she would be. I suggested she go back to work and give us a chance to get her aunt settled comfortably in her room. The woman, even though she clearly cared for her aunt, seemed relieved that I had "given her permission" to go.

"I really should get back to the office," she said appreciatively. "But I'll be back tonight, with my husband. We're very worried about Aunt Mel."

Inside the semiprivate room, the small army mustered to get

the frail woman from the gurney to the hospital bed had apparently made some progress—in the last few minutes I had heard no noises coming from the room. But no people had come out either.

I was more than a little curious as to what was taking them so long, since I knew my cohorts were well trained in dealing with out-of-control patients. Besides, Nancy, like Dolly, weighed enough to overpower almost any patient. The police officers, both over six feet tall, were built like athletes. Rose was the only small person in the room, other than the patient, and she was fast on her feet. The paramedics were no weaklings either. They, too, had training in gentle but firm handling of hysterical or crazed people. The ruckus I had been hearing periodically resounding from the room told me that getting Melissa from the gurney to the high hospital bed had not been a by-the-book procedure.

Finally, when nearly an hour had passed, Dolly, Rose, and Nancy emerged from the room. My coworkers looked a mess, one with her sleeve torn nearly off of her uniform, and all three with their hair badly mussed. The sheepish-looking police officers and paramedics followed. They were shaking their heads and showing signs of genuine relief that the chore was done at last.

They gathered around the nursing station, and the nurses loudly proclaimed that the woman was possessed with a powerful malevolent spirit. The four men, who now joined the nurses in resting on any available chair or table low enough to sit on, did not dispute this particular diagnosis.

As proof, Dolly was demonstrating how the ninety-pound patient had tossed both of the much larger women across the room before her bed restraints could be applied. Melissa had held them at bay and fought them off each time they approached her. When they thought they had a firm hold on her frail body to make the transfer from the gurney to the bed, she had slipped out of their clutches with lightning speed. If Nancy or Dolly or Rose did manage to pin her down, she demonstrated superhuman strength and heaved them away.

Finally, with the policemen and paramedics handling the bed straps, and the three women lifting the kicking, twisting Melissa, all seven of them had been able to complete the transfer and hold the woman long enough to affix the straps to her wrists, ankles, and, for extra measure, her waist.

"That was the most powerful evil spirit I've seen in a long time," Rose said, her large eyes reflecting the horrific sights she had just witnessed. Rose warned everyone within earshot that this particular spirit possession was a threat to any person who came near the old woman. The men departed the unit in a hurry, as if they did not want to wait to see, leaving Dolly, Rose, Nancy, and me to contend with whatever was in that room.

I was alarmed by the sight of my coworkers and the things they were saying about this old woman. "How could such a thing be happening?" I wondered aloud.

"Deborah, every human being has a spiritual side as well as a physical one," Dolly explained. "Both sides require sustenance. For the spiritual side that nourishment is love and attention. For the physical one it is food, liquids, warmth, and shelter. If there is a shortage of any of these, the person's life will get out of balance. That's what happened with Melissa T. Both sides failed to get the refueling they needed. She is going to require as much spiritual nourishment as she does physical and medical attention."

"How do we accomplish *that*?" I asked. I knew the admitting physician had given orders for the treatment of her physical and medical needs.

"Rose, Nancy, and I are preparing to hold a prayer circle around Melissa's bed. You're welcome to join us," Dolly replied. Before I agreed, I checked the old woman's chart to make sure she had been well dosed with the prescribed tranquilizing drugs. Dolly assured me that the patient was well sedated, at least for the time being.

We all entered her room, and I glanced over to see what appeared to be a sleeping, very old woman. Even in sleep there was an almost hateful scowl on her face. Although the heavy dose of tranquilizing drugs had knocked her out, she still looked wild and dangerous to me, despite her tiny body.

I could not reconcile her size with the description of what had transpired in the room. But the account had been told by coworkers I trusted and vouched for by two law officers and two trained medical EMT personnel. These seven people would have absolutely no reason to want to try to fool me with such a yarn, and, of course, none of them had an extra hour to spend getting one little old lady into a hospital bed.

The story was true, but there was no logical explanation in any of my psych textbooks for this kind of supernatural strength coming from a very ill, very old, very frail person.

While I pondered this puzzle, I followed the lead of my three coworkers. I had no experience with Native American prayer circles or praying over patients. To me, one's relationship with the Creator was a private and personal matter. In the past, I had always left such matters to the individual patient's own religious representative. Yet here I was, participating in a prayer circle ceremony.

The simplicity of the ritual was both touching and sobering. We gathered around the bed where Melissa lay restrained. Dolly reached out to take Nancy's hand, then Nancy took Rose's hand, Rose took mine, and, finally to close the circle, I reached across the sleeping woman to take Dolly's other hand.

I expected to hear some special type of incantation, but my teachers simply bowed their heads. If any one of them was saying a prayer or chanting, it was done in silence. I also bowed my head. The simple energy of the union of hands seemed to be all that was necessary. The pulse-beat of Dolly's hand in my right hand and from Rose's hand in my left became the only sense of movement. No sound came from anywhere on the unit. It was as if every one of our patients was cooperating in Melissa's spiritual treatment by doz-ing off for a late afternoon nap. The pulsing rhythm of the hands we held in the circle intensified as we stood in silence. Time seemed to stand still. Later I glanced at my watch and found that the prayer circle ceremony had lasted almost thirty minutes.

During the course of that week, we would repeat the prayer circle ceremony over Melissa's sleeping body at least once a day, and more often if our schedules allowed. At the same time, she was receiving fluids and nourishment intravenously and being forced, with medications, to sleep.

Each day I saw small changes in her. First, her color improved, then her vital signs, which we monitored closely.

But I noticed something else. The scowl on her lips gradually went away and was replaced by a slight smile. Her wild look faded into a serene, almost childlike demeanor. Instead of appearing dan-gerous, she now seemed innocent. The deep, tortured, drug-induced sleep I had noticed the first several days after she was placed in the bed now appeared rhythmic and restful.

I knew as long as Melissa was kept on her medications she would be fine, but I feared what would happen when they had to be withdrawn. For now she was okay. On my way out the door for a long weekend to cram for an exam in one of my graduate courses, I looked in on the sleeping woman.

I returned to work the following Tuesday morning. As I entered the unit, a petite elderly lady in a starched print dress walked by and asked, "Can you tell me where I go for breakfast?" I showed her where the dining area was located and informed her that breakfast trays would be served shortly.

Then I turned to the night-shift nurse for the report. "Who was that?"

"That's Melissa T. from 124A," the nurse said nonchalantly. "I thought she was your patient."

"Who?" I was stunned.

"Melissa T. in 124A," she repeated. "She buzzed us about five A.M. this morning and announced that she was ready to get up for a shower. She bathed and dressed herself in the clothes her family brought for her this past weekend."

I stopped short and wheeled around to see the old woman walking, hesitantly but with determination, toward the dining area. At that moment, Dolly came in for work.

"You won't believe what I just saw," I blurted to Dolly, and then rushed to tell her that Melissa was in the dining area under her own steam, waiting for breakfast. "Can you believe it? She looks like a new woman!"

"Ain't life grand?" Dolly said sardonically.

"Well, I can hardly believe it," I replied.

"Believe it, girlfriend," the stoic Cherokee nurse said. "We didn't hold those prayer circle ceremonies for nothing."

Later in our conversation in the closet-size medicine room, Dolly, Rose, and I discussed Melissa T's miraculous recovery.

"That was the worst case of spirit possession I've seen around here," Rose volunteered.

Dolly agreed.

"Spirit possession! What are you two talking about?" I almost shouted my anger. "The old woman came in here in an acute confusional state. She probably had an underlying case of psychotic depression with paranoid delusions. She was hallucinating when they picked her up. She may even have some form of dementia that has gone untreated."

Dolly and Rose's shaman example of a malevolent spirit possession flew in the face of all the scientific and medical knowledge about aging and depression in the elderly that I had been studying in my psychology courses.

Both women just looked at me. They were grinning, and that made me even more angry.

Finally Dolly said, "Okay, then, what textbook explains how a ninety-pound woman can toss three women, two paramedics, and two policemen around like plastic dolls? I didn't read about that in any of *my* nursing textbooks, and I didn't read about it in my college physics courses either."

She quickly added that the modern medicine regimen we had used on Melissa had certainly been a big factor in healing her body and resting her brain. But she challenged me again.

"How did the old lady sound when you talked to her this morning?" Dolly asked.

"She was lucid and cheerful," I admitted. "She told me she was starving, and really wolfed down her eggs and toast. She seemed eager to talk to me about how she got here and when she could go home."

"And which one of our wonderful drugs do you credit for the change?" Dolly did not wait for a reply. "Do you remember the madwoman we had snarling like a dog in 124A just one week ago?"

I was stumped for an answer and I knew it. The sleeping drugs helped; the intravenous feedings helped. But it was too big a medical leap to explain what seemed like a complete mental turnaround in such a short time, just from the antidepressants we were administering.

"I suggest you think about it for a day or two and then we'll talk about it." Dolly took up her tray of pills and headed toward one of the patient rooms. "Weigh your scientific facts against the knowledge you have acquired here about the spirit elders and how we have told you they operate within the world of the living—especially among the elderly. Try using your intuitive senses instead of your common sense."

By the time Dolly brought up the subject of possession two days later, I was eager to talk to her, because I had drawn a blank pondering all the improbabilities by myself. She reminded me of our conversation about the needs of a person's spiritual side and physical side. She insisted that the prayer circle ceremonies we performed drove out the malevolent spirit that had taken up residence inside the old woman. Once it was gone, she experienced a rapid recovery.

"But it could have been the IVs too," I interjected, weakly now.

"Where do you read on the bottle 'For Restoring Sanity'? I guess I missed that part," Dolly insisted. "That was her physical nourishment, and those interventions did help her body recover and her mind begin to function. When her demon-beset spirit was contacted by our circle of prayers and caring, it was nourished too. Without that, some people can be kept alive on IVs and drugs for a long, long time without ever improving."

"I'm still not sure I accept the possession thing," I ventured. "The medical care surely wouldn't do anything to help Melissa T.'s broken spirit. And it wouldn't rid her spirit of the darkness that surrounded it and put her here in the first place. It's the part about the effects of the darkness that is giving me the problems."

"The darkness that engulfed her life became a breeding ground for the malignant spirits," Dolly said with a steady gaze into my eyes. "Those spirits are always in search of empty souls—that is the darkness. In the case of old people, they move right in, set up camp, and begin sending poisonous messages: *You are old . . . you are useless . . . you are alone . . . nobody wants you around any more . . . you're in the way*.

"Where do you think those classic messages come from? No human beings say such things to them—that is, no *decent* human beings. They don't read it in books or newspapers. But they get the messages loud and clear from somewhere. Soon their spirits are broken, and you know the rest. You see them hauled into this unit on gurneys and in wheelchairs every day. Tell me these aren't demons from somewhere, girlfriend!"

For the next several days, I thought about what Dolly had told me. I made a special effort to spend as much of my free time as possible with Melissa T. I think I was unconsciously studying her, waiting to see the effects of her medicine wear off and her reversion to a wild screaming woman. But it didn't happen. Melissa T. grew stronger every day, and the lower the medication dosages she received, the better she seemed.

Every afternoon when my other patients had been cared for and were either napping or sitting in the day room, involved in whatever activity they were capable of, I dropped by Melissa T.'s room for a chat or just to sit with her for a while. When the weather permitted, we would go into the small patio garden adjoining the unit for our talks.

I soon realized that Melissa T. reminded me of my now-deceased elderly cousin Amelia. They both had naturally auburn hair in their advanced years. My cousin Amelia, like almost everyone else in my extended family, had been so much older than I that she would have been the age of most children's grandmothers. For me, she became a surrogate grandmother. She always seemed to have that extra time for me that my mother did not. Amelia had time to teach me things like proper etiquette and diction. She told me the importance of keeping up with current events. During presidential election years she enjoyed explaining the platforms of each political candidate to me. This made me feel important, like I was a person, not just a child.

Amelia spent hours listening to me talk about my dreams. She encouraged me to explore places outside of my small Tennessee hometown. "Meet people who can introduce you to new ideas and new ways of doing things. It will help keep you young, long after your peers have given up on life," she would say.

Melissa T. was saying many of the same things.

I enjoyed talking to her. In some quiet way, I felt that I was passing on to this old woman a gift I had received from another old woman so many years earlier—the gift of feeling important to someone.

As I listened to Melissa T., at the age of eighty-eight, talk about her plans for where she would go and what she would do once she was discharged from our unit, I realized that I was learning something about life from this dauntless lady. I was learning how important a person's spirit is, especially at the end of life. Of course, she would never return to her own apartment. We both knew that. We also knew that she would have to maintain herself on some form of medication for the rest of her life. But what she knew that I did not was this: Having plans for a future was just as exciting for her as the dreams of any young person.

After weeks with us in the unit, the day arrived when Melissa T.'s niece would come to inform us that a place had been found for her. The old woman had on more than one occasion confided her worst fears to me, fears that her independence would be taken away and that she would have to go into the close confinement of a nursing home. I, too, feared this for her, because I had come to know her independent spirit.

Imagine the thrill for both of us when her niece described where she would be going. The niece and her husband, through a social worker, had secured a room for Melissa at a nearby senior's residential tower. The facility offered private rooms, very small apartments, a central dining room that provided all meals, and an on-site nurse to dole out daily medications. Aunt Mel would be free to come and go as she pleased, even to take a regularly scheduled shopping trip by bus, or to go out with friends or family who might come to drive her. I do not know when I have seen anyone, even a child with a wonderful new toy, so happy, so full of life, as my dear friend when she heard this news.

The experiences with Melissa T. taught me an important lesson. I was coming to a personal place of acceptance that there was indeed more to this cycle of birth-life-death-rebirth than met the eye. I was beginning to recognize that there is a strong spiritual dimension to the last years of life, for the very old and even for the severely demented. This aspect to their lives may make them society's best window into an important part of our true human essence—a part that modern society has lost somewhere along the technological superhighway.

My shaman friends were forcing me to see what was happening to these elderly patients beyond the strictures of medical technology. The older patients, like Aunt Mel, were teaching me things through their spirits that I was not finding in books.

As I watched Melissa and her niece walk out the door, I muttered, "That woman taught me an important lesson. These old people are really unrecognized treasures."

I turned to go back into the neuro-psych unit where twenty others like her sat in various stages of silence waiting for me, for anyone, who would hear their spirit's message. As I turned, my eye caught Dolly watching me, with only the faintest hint of a smile on her lips.

Golden Threads

OVER THE MONTHS, it was Rose who urged me to take these fantastic experiences at a slower pace. One afternoon, soon after Aunt Mel's niece moved her to a new home, we were in the medicine room discussing my progress.

"I think Deborah's next step should be a more gentle visit into the spirit world," Rose said.

I was relieved that someone had noticed how the stress was taking its toll on me, but I did not want to complain about the intensity of my training or back away from the guidance I was receiving. I didn't protest Rose's suggestion either.

Dolly looked a little put out by my acquiescence in what she probably considered a sign of weakness or some character flaw on my part. But she finally agreed that I should be exposed to a different, more serene side of the spiritual realm. She suggested I focus my attention on a male patient who had recently been admitted to the unit. Actually, my next lesson centered on a couple. Stephen Z.'s wife came to the Plantation every day to visit her severely demented husband.

"We've been married for fifty years," his wife, Barbara, told me the first time we met. "There's no way anyone is going to separate us now."

From his chart, I saw that Stephen Z. was in an advanced stage of Alzheimer's. He had been admitted to our unit for treatment of sleep deprivation, which had left him agitated. His inability to sleep and his agitated behaviors had become too much for his wife to manage at home.

Stephen Z. appeared to be an unusually happy person, although he was oblivious to the world around him and everyone in it—including his wife. Nonetheless, she came to the hospital daily to spend her every waking hour with him.

Barbara's voice filled with pride whenever she spoke about her husband. He had been an exceptionally brilliant mechanical engineer, responsible for contributing major work to some of the landmark skyscrapers around the world. The couple had reared two lovely daughters, and in their retirement years had traveled the world together.

Their daughters were frequent visitors to the neuro-psych unit too. When the family was together, they seemed to form a circle of love around themselves. They always included Stephen in their conversations, despite his inability to recognize any of them and his ongoing stream of chatter, which usually had nothing to do with the topic of conversation at that moment.

As for our role with Stephen's case, other than providing the palliative care and supportive treatment—vitamins and sleep-inducing drugs—there was nothing medically that could be done to improve his condition. The unit's social worker was trying to find a permanent residential placement for him, once he was discharged from the Plantation.

Stephen's wife had kept him at home with her for quite a number of years after he was diagnosed with Alzheimer's. But he was beginning to display numerous behavioral and personality changes that were making it increasingly difficult for her to care for him alone. Rose told me he had been treated at the Plantation on one other occasion before I joined the staff. His disease had progressed significantly since that last admission.

His wife was fearful for him and completely unwilling to be separated. Finding a facility where Stephen could receive round-the-clock care and Barbara could live close by was no easy assignment for the social worker. Unfortunately, this is a predicament faced by many families, when one member has Alzheimer's and the other aging spouse or loved one is still healthy. Stephen Z. had sufficient means to handle just about any type of long-term care, but finding a facility that would accommodate his needs *and* his wife's, in the early 1990s, was a challenging task.

Stephen's sleep deprivation and the resulting agitation were treated with hypnotics and antianxiety drugs. His condition quickly stabilized, and he slept for the first several days. After receiving the benefits of some much-needed sleep, his agitated behaviors began to subside. Soon he was back to his pleasant, docile self.

Stephen and Barbara's two daughters, who were in their late thirties or early forties, offered to take in their aged mother and father, if that option made sense. But both had families with children at home to tend. And the doctors all concurred that Stephen Z. would need long-term, professional care for the balance of his life.

The daughters visited their father and mother some weekday after-noons and on weekends. They clearly doted on their dad and tried to support and comfort their mother.

Barbara arrived every morning, just after her husband finished breakfast. Her white hair was always curled and coifed, her ensemble stylish and colorful. Her routine was always the same. She shaved Stephen, combed his hair, washed his face and hands, and dressed him in clean clothes—fresh khaki pants and a light sports shirt. Sometimes she added a beige cardigan sweater when she thought he might get cold.

They spent the first part of the morning in his room. Then she would escort him out into the recreation area, where they busied themselves for the rest of the day. When he was unsteady on his feet, she used a wheelchair to transport him to the place that became their private corner of the world.

They sat quietly in the recreation area for hours. Stephen seemed content to find a thread or button on his clothing and entertain himself with it. He would toy with that button for long periods of time or wrap a loose thread around his finger, unwinding it and rewrapping it, over and over again.

He remained stationary in his seat unless Barbara moved him to some other location. She always sat as close to him as possible, on the sofa or in a nearby chair. Even when he underwent a treatment procedure, his wife was never physically far from him. She read magazines or did knitting and needlework to occupy herself. At lunchtime she set up his tray and helped supervise his eating. Because she wanted him to maintain some level of independence, she never attempted to feed him unless he indicated that he wanted her to do so. She got him cleaned up after lunch and then sometimes, on sunny days, they went out onto the patio. This daily routine could be counted on like clockwork. It was Barbara's way of showing love for her husband and continuing to share a life with him. They both seemed to enjoy it. Apparently just being together was enough for them.

Stephen Z. had been in Rose's care on the previous admission, and it was her idea to assign his case to me this time. She and I talked about the relationship that kept Stephen Z. and his wife together for so many years. Rose believed it was the most extraordinary example of husband-and-wife bonding she had ever encountered. She told me Barbara had insisted on caring for her husband at home, despite the fact that his condition had progressively worsened over the past four years. She was willing to do anything necessary to remain by his side.

During quiet times I often slipped into the back of the day room to observe this old couple absorbed in nothing more than their togetherness. Barbara talked to Stephen as if nothing were wrong with him. Occasionally when her voice appeared to register with him, Stephen would stop all activities and look over toward her. With a wide grin on his face, as if he understood the topic of conversation, he would nod, mumble a few words, and then return to the thread that was wrapped around his finger. Barbara acknowledged the momentary connection with a smile.

Sometimes I caught Barbara sitting quietly watching her husband. Occasionally I saw tears rolling down her face. Those were the times she seemed to miss him the most. When the flash of loneliness went away, she would reminisce with him about one of their trips or read to him a letter from a friend.

One afternoon I saw an exchange between them that has been

etched on my heart ever since. Barbara was reading aloud to Stephen. He was tugging at a button on his cardigan. Suddenly, for no apparent reason, he got up from his chair, walked over to where Barbara was reading, and sat down next to her. He put his arm around her waist, glanced into her eyes, and smiled. Then he hugged and kissed her. The stunned Barbara's face lit up—a kiss from her husband! It had been years since she had felt the touch of his lips on her skin. As quickly as it happened, the event was over. Stephen got up from his seat beside her and returned to his wheelchair. Barbara sat quietly and held onto the moment for as long as possible.

This wife's unwavering loyalty was in itself a phenomenon. It made me think deeply about the extraordinary value such a relationship could have on any old person stricken with this condition.

To many casual observers, this might seem like a sad story about the blight of Alzheimer's disease. But there is another overriding factor in this case. Of all the patients assigned to me during my two years on this unit, Stephen Z. was the most consistently happy and serene of any of my patients with dementia. Even though he recognized no one, he expressed appreciation with his eyes and mannerisms for every kindness and assistance rendered. It was as if the love that surrounded him throughout his life was nurturing his spirit during his time of transition.

Barbara told me all she wanted for the two of them was to be together for the remainder of his life and to be reunited with him in the afterlife. She proved her wish was sincere because in the here-and-now she and her husband were inseparable. Over time I began to sense the depth of their bond.

One afternoon, I was observing them in their usual routine of sitting together, oblivious to everyone else around them. Just seeing them gave me a respite from the stresses I encountered with some of the other patients. I was again in a position to observe them without being noticed, as they sat on a sofa, not touching but close enough to reach out to each other. I think Barbara was knitting.

Watching the couple, I felt a strong emotional tug at my heart, remembering the recent kiss I had witnessed. Suddenly a light appeared in the space between them, which gradually brightened as I looked on. At first, I thought it was a shaft of sunlight streaming through the blinds, or perhaps a reflection from a shiny piece of jewelry she was wearing. But the late-afternoon sun was already low in the sky. And Barbara, who rarely wore jewelry, had none on that day.

As I stared harder at the couple, I realized the glow was emanating from them, crossing the space between them through an ethereal web. Golden cords or threads extended outward from their bodies and were woven together in a fine lattice of light. The cords glowed as if they were transmitting some pulsating energy between this husband and wife. Their spirits seemed connected by these delicate threads.

I glanced around to see if anyone else had noticed, but the only people in the room were two old men engrossed in a news report blaring on the TV. I wished at least one of my shamanic coworkers would walk in so she could confirm what I was seeing. But, as usual, I was to have this experience alone, when my mind and heart were focused.

When I mentioned these images of golden threads to Rose, she showed no surprise. She told me the spirits of Stephen Z. and his wife had been joined together by the experiences of love they had shared for so many years. "They have woven a golden cord that will keep them tied together forever—both here and in the afterlife," the gentle woman said.

I continued to observe this phenomenon for the remainder of Stephen Z.'s stay on the unit. Some days there was nothing. Then I would see them together, and suddenly the clear picture of the golden cords between them would flash into my mind.

One day the social worker came into the TV room with a big grin on her face. I watched her talking in an animated way to the couple, waving her hands and pointing north. I saw Barbara stand and embrace the young woman, then turn to Stephen, who was working on a button at the time, and give him a big hug. As usual, he did not respond.

Barbara's first wish had been granted—she would be able to stay with Stephen for the rest of his days. One of their daughters had arranged for a suitable living arrangement, through a contact the social worker had recommended. She had found a small community in the mountains just two hours outside of the city. There Stephen Z. would be cared for in a nursing-home setting, and Barbara could live nearby, in a small cottage on the same grounds. They would remain together to the end. As for Barbara's second wish, I have no doubt at all that their spirits will be together in the next dimension as well.

In the eighteen months since I had joined the staff of the neuropsych unit, I learned that the shaman women held practically every aspect of life sacred. To them life itself is sacred. Thus, there could be no good or bad outcome, just lessons to be learned for spiritual growth. Because of these beliefs, Dolly and Rose, and to a lesser extent Nancy, approached the tragic disabilities besetting these old people as part of the natural order of life.

As caretakers for these patients in this special setting, we were charged with looking after their bodies and providing a nurturing environment to the best of our capabilities. When I began to witness the things going on in the spirit dimension, I naturally felt my responsibilities had been extended.

The events surrounding Aunt Mel and Stephen Z. were paradoxical. I was still having difficulty processing them. A nondemented, healthy Aunt Mel had apparently succumbed to the influences of a malevolent spirit. Stephen Z., a severely demented and physically vulnerable individual, had not. Why? These diametrically opposite manifestations from the spirit world troubled me, and I wanted to see the best outcome for my patients in that realm too. So I demanded an explanation from my three guides.

Their answers were uniform: Love makes all the difference. Its effects are far-reaching.

A loving relationship between a couple and a loving environment among family members and good friends is so powerful and protective that it overcomes all negative events in this life. Love of family and friends even reaches beyond the tangible, into the spirit realm and the world beyond.

Aunt Mel lost too many friends and family too quickly. It weakened her reserves and caused her to become vulnerable to outside influences. Stephen Z. had always been surrounded by his family, with their love and adoration. He never became vulnerable to those influences that Aunt Mel did.

"This protective circle of love is especially important to the quality of life for people suffering from Alzheimer's and the other diseases that can cause dementia—and for the relatives who care for them," Dolly said. "It guides the family members through each day and helps them to cope with the withering process they are forced to watch."

It was true. The aura of love displayed by the wife and children of Stephen Z. was almost palpable, even without the manifestation of the golden web.

My three shamanic friends implied that their belief in the power of love was the basis for the way they treated the patients on the unit. Our time with these people was very limited, and could not change everything that had happened to them in the past. However, at this stage of life, even respect made a powerful difference in the patients' day-to-day mental states. Almost any positive outreach in dealing with the demented elderly had a visible positive return.

Many of the old people we cared for were particularly responsive to this type of ministration, because they had never learned about loving relationships. Others had lost the protective benefits that come with love or had life experiences, over time, that had hardened their hearts.

Dolly explained that some people can start out as loving children and grow into a negative adulthood because of bad experiences along the way. Thus, they enter this critical last stage of life as embittered, angry people. When they are stricken with a disease like Alzheimer's, they have no foundation to help them cope with its ravages and no support system of friends or family. The women believed it was these latter patients who seemed to be in constant conflict and vulnerable to malevolent spirits.

Rose explained that it was necessary for me to recognize the difference as I explored the path into the dimension of the spirit. I had now seen instances of both positive and negative outcomes.

Dolly said she had purposefully directed my attention to some of the more extreme cases on the unit so that I could learn about the vast diversity of spirits in the other dimension. My most recent experience with Stephen Z. was to give me the opportunity to witness the positive power that loving relationships in this life can have on the spiritual dimension.

The result of such spiritual power building supported the mother, supported the father—even though he had Alzheimer's—and provided comfort to the children. It resulted in this family incorporating everyone's needs into the caretaking plan for the father. There was no struggle within the family. There was none of the strife that is seen in many families of Alzheimer's patients. There wasn't the absolute exhaustion and weariness. Certainly the family members, particularly Barbara, were tired because the struggle to remain positive is unending. But for them the experience with the father's Alzheimer's, although painful, was unifying, not shattering.

It did not matter that Stephen Z. didn't recognize them anymore. It mattered that he had a long, loving, intense, highly connected relationship with his wife and with their children. Somehow the quality of that relationship and that connection allowed them to endure the hardships, even to remain happy as a family unit.

Dolly, Rose, Nancy, and I then began to share stories about other families who brought their stresses and anxieties onto the unit. Patients from those families often acted up while their relatives were visiting or reacted badly after they left. They were responding to the tension of the family discord. When I say discord, I'm talking about brothers and sisters, spouses and children openly arguing about topics that should have been resolved elsewhere: *What is to be done with the patient after discharge? How will the property be divided? Who is named in the will? Whose name is on the insurance policies?* I have even had family members—thinking that the elder demented relative cannot understand a word—ask me, "How much longer do you think this old geezer will last?"

Senile dementia, especially the Alzheimer's type, can be the catalyst that draws the worst poisons in a family to the surface—poisons like blame, recrimination, guilt, greed, and even outright cruelty. Or, as in the case of Stephen Z., it can illuminate the foundation, the rock, upon which a strong family relationship is built.

The progressive and irreversible nature of many of these illnesses often exposes family relationships to a glaring hot light that is brighter than the depths of the darkness of the diseases themselves. Unlike sudden death from a heart attack, accident, or even the relatively fast death of some cancers, the senile dementias—like Alzheimer's—force family members to spend a lot of time together in retrospective conversations. They have to deal with far more than just the physical loss of an elderly loved one. The nature of these diseases seems to force family members to examine their relationships.

This is why the changing makeup of the family unit in the industrialized world will soon become even more problematic than it is now. Except for holiday celebrations, it is rare for several generations of one family to visit or spend any extended time together. If this trend continues, the current aging population will be losing the traditional family networks its parents and grandparents had to fall back on. Eventually this group will be forced to rely on strangers or paid healthcare workers for its end-of-life care.

High divorce rates are adding to the sense of disconnection

within many family networks. Increasingly that sense of disconnection, among members of a society that glorifies youth, produces a generalized belief system that devalues anyone beyond a given age. For those elderly people who develop dementia and are no longer able to "carry their load," the outlook is bleak.

"There is a growing perception that people with dementia have nothing to offer," said Dolly. "But that is simply not true." The nurse's voice was charged with a controlled anger.

"Deborah, we wanted to expose you to Stephen and Barbara Z. and their golden threads because we wanted you to see how important the bonding between people can be. Our cultures hold that everyone in a tribe is connected to everyone else. The tribe raises the children, not a single mother and father. Every child is the responsibility of the tribe, the community. And everyone is responsible for the elderly at the other end of life."

She caught her breath and continued. "This connection does not end with death. When people share life together, their spirits meet again in the afterlife. The circle is never broken, never ending. The spirits remain a part of the living. There is an unbroken communion."

The experience with Stephen Z. and his family proved to me that this connectedness that Dolly, Rose, and Nancy talked about was available to everyone, not just to those Native Americans and other groups who adhere to their tribal bonds.

This example of the power of bonding, of love, was strong and lasting. It provided me with a glimpse into a bright side of the spirit dimension that served as a shining relief from the more stressful steps along the path I traveled with my shaman friends. My co-workers told me I was making progress in my efforts to accept that there were alternative ways of viewing life and death.

"A person does not have to reject the reality of the apparent to accept that there is also a spiritual dimension to the world around us," Rose said.

It was now time for me to move along with my spiritual training. However, nothing I had witnessed so far could have prepared me for the challenge ahead.

Symphony of Spirits

IF THERE WAS a test of my progress on this journey, it
came in the form of the next lesson my shaman coworkers chose
for me. Dolly and Rose suggested I work with a patient who
returned to the neuro-psych unit on many occasions. She was an
eighty-four-year-old woman suffering from advanced Huntington's
disease.

The woman was wheeled by an admitting clerk onto the unit
strapped into a wheelchair. Even though she was secured in the
chair at the waist, her bony arms and legs were flopping about in
all directions.

Dolly rushed to meet them and immediately began trying to
calm the old woman, soothingly calling her name, Ethel, and telling
her how pleased everyone was to see her again. We took the wheelchair and its passenger from the clerk and headed to a private room.
Dolly chatted away about how much fun *we*—meaning the woman
and the staff—were going to have now that she was back at the
Plantation for a "visit." I removed the strap from around her waist,
and together we lifted her gangly body from the chair to the bed.

"We don't need to strap you into the bed now, do we, Ethel?" Dolly's voice and reassuring presence seemed to have already calmed the old woman down.

I had seen her on the unit at least twice since joining the staff, and I knew she was a favorite with the nurses.

"Ethel and I are old friends. She's been around here as long as I have," Dolly cooed as she tucked the sheets around her patient. Surprisingly, in just a few minutes the old woman had stopped thrashing about in the bed and dropped off to sleep.

"Let's get a cup of coffee so Rose and I can fill you in on this patient," Dolly suggested, taking my arm and leading me to the nurse's station. Rose joined us and they quickly told me the old woman's history.

Although Ethel V. was the widow of a wealthy southern gentleman, her life story resembled a classic Greek tragedy. Her case and much of her personal history were familiar to Dolly and Rose, because they had cared for her frequently when she was admitted to our unit to stabilize her combative behaviors and sleep-cycle irregularities. I vaguely remembered her, but my coworkers brought me up to date.

Her life of southern wealth and gentility had done her little good because it had been spent as a battered wife in an era when women dared not leave an abusive husband. The beatings finally ended when her husband died. Apparently, her late husband had targeted many of his blows at her head. Her medical history indicated that she had suffered a number of concussions over the years. Dolly made it clear she thought the husband's untimely death was the best thing that could have happened. But Ethel V. did not have long to enjoy her inheritance or her delivery from her husband's cruel hand, because a few years later she was diagnosed with the progressively degenerating condition known as Huntington's disease.

During her forty-year marriage, Ethel V. had been a foster mother to forty-two children. Her husband apparently had shown more philanthropy in bringing unwanted children into their home for Ethel to take care of than in nurturing a loving relationship with his wife. Unfortunately for Ethel, not one of their foster children ever repaid her kindness by visiting her in the nursing home where she permanently resided when not a patient on our unit. They did not even come to the Plantation to visit when her condition became grave. Dolly and Rose questioned if they even knew what had become of Ethel once they left her home. What little attention the old woman did receive was doled out by her two spinster nieces.

During this admission, Dolly and Rose decided that Ethel V. would be my patient. In assigning Ethel to me, Dolly used the excuse that her caseload was too full. That was the rationale, but she and Rose later confided that they wanted me to spend some time with the old woman to expand my understanding of the spirit realm.

From the beginning it was clear that Ethel V. would have preferred to have one of her old friends take care of her. She felt comfortable with Dolly and Rose and, to the best of her ability, let everyone know she did not particularly want me to be her nurse. When I tried to perform the simplest of tasks, like taking a blood pressure, she would screech and hiss at me. If Dolly or Rose entered the room during the procedure, she instantly became a model patient, cooperating with their every request.

The staff treated Ethel V. like the unit's mascot. Despite her limited cognitive and physical abilities, she had developed a rapport with nurses from all of the shifts. It was as if she were a member of the family. They babied her. They let her do things that other patients were not allowed to do, such as spend the afternoon in the nurse's station in a wheelchair. She was even allowed to sit in the nurse's station with us while we did our chart work.

Besides the fact she was a regular patient, I think another reason the nurses paid special attention to Ethel V. was because they felt particularly moved by the cruelty she had endured throughout her life. In the nurses' opinion, the treatment prescribed for her condition wasn't much kinder.

When I first started at the Plantation, I was surprised to learn that the doctors used electroconvulsive therapy (ECT) to reset the neurochemical formulation of the brain in some dementia patients. Ethel was one of those patients. She received a series of up to twelve individual ECT treatments spread over the course of several weeks each time she was admitted.

The two nieces who were her legal guardians had placed her in a local nursing home. They constantly complained about the cost of having Ethel V. at our facility. Each time she was admitted to our unit, they were forced to pay full price to maintain her room at the nursing home, even when she was with us for weeks at a time. Thus, they wanted her treated at the Plantation and returned to the nursing home as quickly as possible. It was a vicious cycle. Ethel V.'s disruptive and combative behaviors would flare up and the nursing home staff would have her sent to us for ECT treatment. The treatments stabilized her for a while, and she would be sent back until the next episode.

Dolly told me that Ethel's substantial estate was paying for her

care, but the nieces were resentful that the double cost of hospi-
talization and nursing-home fees was eating away at their expected
inheritance. They had gained legal control of their aunt's estate by
having a local county judge declare her incompetent and name them
as her guardians. Before that, Ethel had lived in her twenty-room
mansion assisted by servants and paid visiting nurses. Once the
nieces were granted control of her estate, they immediately rushed
her off to a local nursing home. This had been several years ago
and, to their chagrin, according to Dolly, Ethel had survived much
longer than anyone had expected.

Clinically, Ethel V. was a very sick woman when she was admitted to our unit this last time. She was suffering from an upper-
respiratory infection. Her frail-looking body was showing the long-
term effects of living with a degenerative neurological condition.
She had protracted mood swings and was having difficulty with
her speech, her ability to swallow, and the movement of her
extremities.

Huntington's disease was slowly taking its toll on her cognitive
abilities. Her ability to communicate was better on some days and
worse on others. Because each ECT treatment left her disoriented
and foggy, some days she could not recognize anyone or speak
coherently. When she could not make herself or her needs clear to
her old friends Dolly and Rose, we knew she was having one of her
very rough days.

Even though Dolly assigned me to Ethel V., neither she nor
Rose ever completely gave up participating in her care.

"I'll let you take care of Ethel, but Rose and I will be checking
in on her from time to time. She's already had more than her share

of trouble in life," Dolly said when she assigned me the case. "I'll check in with her to make sure everything is okay and to let her know we're still here for her."

I apparently got a satisfactory rating from Ethel, because after a few days I was assigned to be her primary nurse for the duration of this lengthy stay. She remained on the unit for two or three months because, unlike prior admissions, she did not respond well to the treatments she was receiving for her upper-respiratory infection and her erratic behaviors. In fact, after the first couple of ECT treatments she had what can only be described as a near-death experience.

It was my duty, as Ethel's primary nurse, to deliver her to the second-floor treatment room, where her ECT procedures were administered. Each time she had to be placed on a gurney and wheeled out of the unit, down a long hall, and up to the second floor, where her psychiatrist and an anesthesiologist were waiting. I left the room immediately after depositing Ethel with the doctors. Even though I knew she would be heavily sedated and oblivious to the entire ECT procedure, I still did not like to watch any aspect of it. After a two-hour stay in the recovery room, Ethel would be returned to the unit and her private room.

Ethel was not responding to the ECT treatments as well as she had in the past. For several days following the first few treatments her eyes appeared vacant. She would stay awake only long enough to mumble a few incoherent words and then fall back into a deep sleep. Her medications had to be crushed and mixed into chocolate pudding, her favorite food. She was having more and more difficulty swallowing. Getting her to drink liquids was a battle. Finally she became so dehydrated we had to put her on intravenous fluids.

The first extraordinary incident occurred right after one of her ECT treatments.

Ethel was supposed to be sleeping off the effects of the sedative the anesthesiologist had given her. But when I passed her room, I heard voices that sounded like a conversation coming from inside.

When I walked in I saw no one. The fluorescent light was off. The drapes were closed tightly, and only a small night-light illuminated the room. I was somewhat surprised to hear her talking. She usually did not wear her false teeth, and when she tried to talk without them, she was almost impossible to understand. Now her speech was crystal clear.

The clarity of her voice alone would have been enough to cause me to stop and pay attention. But as my eyes adjusted to the light of the partially darkened room, I saw several misty shapes on each side of her bed.

My entry into the room did not alter what was going on around Ethel's bed, nor did it interrupt her conversation. In a low but audible voice she was talking with these forms, calling them by name. I quickly understood they were relatives from a much earlier time, when her life was filled with happiness.

The images were indistinct. They were more transparent than any of the figures I had witnessed before.

These were not completely formed entities, but rather gauzy in appearance. As I stared at the images on either side of the bed, I realized that I only saw their upper bodies. If they had legs touching the floor I did not notice, nor did it seem to make any difference. The laws of gravity obviously did not apply to them.

I was sure Ethel V. was talking to kin because she was using family names, like Momma, Paw, and nicknames of siblings and cousins. She was addressing them in a girlish, almost childlike voice. I am not sure if I heard any response from them, but I could sense that they were encouraging her to come with them, assuring her it was time to leave this' place.

Ethel's bed was partially cranked up so her head and shoulders were raised slightly. Her eyes were open, and she was looking from one figure to the next as she spoke to them.

I say she "spoke," but I am not at all sure it was an auditory conversation. It was a dialogue between her and the apparitions around her. But after thinking about this incident many, many times, I cannot be sure Ethel's mouth was actually moving when she spoke. I eavesdropped on what was being "said," or at least the thoughts within the conversation.

I had completed grief training workshops with Dr. Kübler-Ross and had been exposed to the spirit world several times at the Plantation, so I accepted this phenomenon as part of the process. The experience wasn't rattling my nerves as others had. At the moment I felt more concern for my patient than for what I was witnessing. Ethel's breathing was very shallow. There were long pauses between each breath. The pauses were getting longer and longer as the seconds passed. Years of nursing practice told me she would expire shortly if this pattern continued.

I was conscious of Ethel's physical needs above and beyond the strange thing that was going on around her. Only a few months before, the presence of multiple apparitions would have stopped me cold in my tracks. Now Ethel's shallow, almost nonexistent breathing alarmed me more. I moved quickly across the room toward the figures beside the bed. When I came to a spot that would have brought me into contact with the figures on the right side, there was no resistance. As suddenly as I had seen the figures, they disappeared. I took Ethel's bony, wrinkled wrist in my hand, feeling for a pulse. There was only the faintest beat. I tried to arouse her by grabbing both of her shoulders, shaking her upper body, and calling out her name.

Just then Rose came into the room.

"Ethel has company," she said.

"I know," I replied. "I saw them too."

Rose gave me a quizzical look. "Her nieces are in the lobby," she said.

"What?" I was puzzled. "I mean her family was here, just now."

"No, they're waiting in the lobby," Rose said, then hesitated. Her large eyes grew wide. "Oh! You mean *they* were here . . . the others."

"Yes," I said. "She almost left with them. Ethel's in bad shape. I think she almost slipped away from us just now."

Rose joined me at the bedside and we listened to Ethel's shallow and irregular breathing for a few moments. Gradually it became stronger. The crisis seemed to have passed.

Within seconds of Ethel's return to normal, two women entered the room. One was in her early fifties. The other was older, perhaps in her late fifties or early sixties. Both women were starkly dressed in dark cotton dresses. Their hair was done up in tight buns. Rose introduced them to me as Ethel's nieces.

"How is Aunt Ethel? Her doctor called us yesterday and told us she was doing better." The older woman was doing the talking.

"I'm not so sure about that," I said. "She was having some trouble breathing a short while ago. She's better now. She just went back to sleep."

Rose told the nieces that Ethel still had two more ECT treatments scheduled before her release.

"Do you really think she needs them?" the younger woman snapped. "I mean she . . . uh . . . looks the same. She's just very old. . . . Can't she get along without the last two treatments? They're so expensive."

"We're the guardians of her estate, you know," the older woman piped in. "We have to make sure her money lasts. My sister and I moved into her house after she went to the nursing home— to look after her things and to save money. There are so many expenses. We have to stretch the money as far as we can, so there will be enough for all of us." In so many words, she was trying to make it clear to me and Rose that they expected to have enough money left in the estate's funds, following Ethel's death, to take care of them for the rest of their lives.

I could barely remain civil after what I had witnessed in Ethel's room before their arrival. But I caught myself. It was not my place to pass judgment on this or any patient's family. I didn't relish the thought of Ethel undergoing any more ECT treatments either, but my reasons had nothing to do with the expense.

After a few more minutes of idle conversation, the nieces left. They handed me a bag of what they described as Aunt Ethel's favorite, homemade chocolate cookies for her to eat when she was "feeling better."

Because her medical condition had become so unstable, the doctor agreed to delay the next ECT treatment until Ethel had improved.

Once past this crisis, she began to complain or cry whenever we tried to get her out of bed and into her wheelchair. She did not want to leave her room for any reason.

A few days later when her condition had improved, Ethel received another ECT treatment. When I left work Friday, she was still sleeping from the exhausting procedure.

Over the weekend she took another turn for the worse. When I arrived at the Plantation Monday morning, the night-shift nurse told me Ethel had slept almost the entire weekend. The staff tried to rouse her several times without success. Her vital signs had slipped to critically low levels.

After I prepared my tray of morning medications, I dropped in to check on Ethel. As I approached the room I could hear her voice. Again, her speech was clearer than it could possibly have been for a person in her condition. I thought, *She must have improved overnight.*

But when I entered the room, she was sleeping.

I closed the door and went over to the foot of her bed. I studied her sleeping figure for a long while. I began to realize that I had grown as fond of this old lady as had the other nurses on the unit. While she apparently was often cantankerous at her nursing home, she graced us with a sweet, appreciative disposition when anyone showed her the slightest kindness. There probably had been too few kindnesses in her troubled life.

I noticed Ethel's breathing was still labored and decided that she must have dropped back to sleep just after I heard her talking.

Then she began to speak again. I thought she was talking in her sleep, but her whispered words were crisp and youthful. I listened hard to catch pieces of what she was saying.

"Momma, is that you? Poppa, tell Mom to wait for me. Uncle John . . . Uncle John, can I play just a little longer? Zach . . . Zach . . . tell Momma to take me too! It's my turn to go!"

As I stood at the foot of the bed, figures similar to those I had seen the previous week began to materialize on either side. They posed beside Ethel as naturally as thousands of bedside visitors I had seen with patients throughout my career. I was standing within an arm's length of these apparitions. They seemed to pay no attention to my presence.

Ethel continued to talk. Her eyelids occasionally fluttered, as if she were trying to wake up but could not. I sensed the ethereal visitors were telling her to come along and leave the hospital with them. They seemed to be assuring Ethel that there was a much better option for her than returning to the nursing home or to anything else available to her now.

Then I thought Ethel had finally awakened and was trying to sit up in bed. I saw her clearly, pale and thin, trying to rise. I wanted to help her but felt glued to the floor. It was so real an image of an old woman struggling to raise herself while the visitors did nothing that I wanted to shout to them to help her.

Then it struck me. Ethel was lying flat on her back. I could see her through the image of the entity I saw rising up from her in the bed. The pale presence was an identical, watery shadow of the real woman. It was rising from her body and was reaching out to the visitors. All the time I could hear Ethel's voice continuing to talk to them.

My years of training and experience overrode any fascination with what I was seeing. A sense of panic swept through my body. Ethel V. was dying right in front of me. Her spirit was leaving her body.

I shouted for help at the top of my voice. I wanted someone, anyone to come to the room. The door was closed, so I doubted that Nancy or Rose or Dolly could hear me call out. I rushed to the side of the bed, half expecting to run up against the mysterious visitors. But again, there was no contact as I reached the spot where they had been just moments before.

Ethel was not breathing. I felt for a pulsing sensation in the carotid artery in her neck and could not find it. I began pushing on her chest with the crossed palms of my hands in smooth, evenly timed strokes.

Miraculously, Dolly and Rose came rushing into the room.

"What's happening?" Dolly shouted.

"Ethel just stopped breathing. She's dying!" I called out between compressions.

"Take it easy, Deborah." Dolly seemed to be trying to calm me as she moved to respond to the crisis at hand. "Rose, get Ethel's doctor on the unit, STAT!"

Suddenly Ethel took a giant gulp of air, opened her eyes, and smiled toothlessly at Dolly, who was now peering right into her face.

Her steel-gray eyes turned toward me. She gave me a glare of disapproval so withering that I almost took a step backward. I stopped applying pressure to her bony chest and pulled my hands away.

It was as if she had been fully conscious and aware of everything going on in the room during the preceding minutes and was extremely upset that I had interfered.

Ethel's doctor came, examined her, and pronounced that she was "just fine for an old lady in her condition." Dolly and I remained in Ethel's room long after quitting time, talking about what had happened that afternoon before she rushed into the room.

"Dolly, she was dying. I'm sure of it."

"She probably was," Dolly agreed.

"Her family came to take her. I saw them—and I saw her spirit climbing out of her body to go with them," I stammered.

"What happened then?"

"I couldn't let her go with them. I started resuscitating her. That's when you and Rose came in," I replied.

I had thought I was doing the right thing. That's what I was trained to do—save lives. I thought Ethel would be happy I saved her life. But she wasn't. When she came around and began talking again, she was furious with me. She kept saying over and over "Damn you! Leave me alone! Get away from me. Damn you!"

"Why is she so mad at me?" I was only trying to help her. I directed my lame defense at Dolly but hoped Ethel V. understood too.

"Deborah, girlfriend, don't you understand what you did?" Dolly replied. "I thought you would by now!"

"Understand what?" I said. I didn't have a clue.

"You pulled her back. She was ready to go. She was on her way."

"Pulled her back from where? What are you talking about?"

"You pulled her from the spirit world back to this one. And

for what?" Dolly was determined to make me understand what I had done.

". . . so that she could keep on living." My voice began to quiver. Something was happening. It felt like the very core of my soul was being twisted inside out and turned upside-down and around. I could hardly catch my breath.

"So that she could keep on living." Dolly repeated my words. "And what does *living* mean for her?"

"Well . . . uh . . . getting more shock treatments . . . and then going back to the nursing home."

The reality of what I had done began to set in. *Ethel's spirit was ready to cross over to the other side. It was on its way. My fear of letting her go got in the way. It caused me to do something that pulled her back to this world. Now she would have to endure more unpleasantness.* I was utterly and totally devastated when I realized the consequences of my actions—actions that were driven by my fears, not Ethel's wishes.

Dolly watched every muscle in my face move as I went through that chain of thoughts. She could tell from the look on my face that I recognized what I had done. I understood why Ethel was so angry with me.

At that point there was nothing I could do to change the outcome of my actions. Ethel would have to finish her ECT treatments and then return to the nursing home. There she would have to wait for another visit from her relatives in the spirit realm. As for me, I would be forced to live with the knowledge of what I had done to this old woman.

When I could finally catch my breath, something deep in my soul was different. That "something" would not become clear until a few days later. Ethel had one more lesson to teach me.

When her vital signs returned to some semblance of normal, Ethel's doctor decided to resume her ECT treatments. I never wanted so badly to contradict a doctor's order in my life. But I knew better than that. I said nothing.

TEN

Transition Angel

LOSING SO MANY of my relatives in such a short period of time years earlier had left a deep scar on my soul. Letting go of anyone I cared about had become a real struggle for me. I cared about Ethel. *I* didn't want to let her pass on into the spirit world. *I* wanted to keep her here in this world. My years of training and experience had taught me how to accomplish that goal. I knew how to save lives. Nowhere in my training had anyone taught me how to let go. Despite my recent glimpses into the world of spirits and the death-and-dying training from Elisabeth Kübler-Ross herself, my own broken spirit would not allow me to give up and let this old woman cross over into the afterlife. Part of that "something different in my soul" was a realization that I had been selfish. My actions had been driven by *my need* to hold on to her, not by *her wish* to be left free to go on into the spirit world.

Once her vital signs were stabilized, Ethel V.'s next ECT treatment was set to resume. Ethel still looked extremely worn out. Her sunken eyes conveyed a sense of deep weariness. Her wiry gray hair was frayed and stood out in all directions, like it had been plugged into a wall socket.

The day for the next ECT treatment came all too quickly. I gave Ethel the preprocedure sedative as scheduled. Her skin was pale and cool. Beneath the crisp hospital sheets, I could see that her breathing was still very uneven. I grew more and more concerned for her ability to withstand the procedure that would take place later that morning. At just that moment Dolly and Rose walked into Ethel's room. Was it serendipity, divine intervention, or the spirit elders at work? I will never know. But memories of the events that transpired after their arrival still give me great comfort, even years later.

We discussed my concerns for Ethel's well-being. Rose and Dolly believed that Ethel's spirit, as well as her body, had been weakened over the course of this stay. They recommended we perform a prayer circle ceremony for Ethel before her ECT treatment that morning. I quickly agreed.

"I'll go get Nancy," Rose said as she darted out the door.

Dolly and I both checked Ethel's vital signs again. We were trying to give each other some reassurance that Ethel's condition was stable enough for the upcoming procedure. The numbers were acceptable. There was no reason to request another cancellation. Still, we were both very concerned. At that moment I could not help but recall my efforts to save Ethel's life just days earlier. I felt a strong sense of guilt.

Dolly and Rose had not chided me for what they clearly thought of as my interference with the spirits the week before. In fact, we had hardly spoken of the incident. It was not the shaman way to criticize an acolyte. A misstep in dealing with the other world had its own disciplining results, notably the loss of progress along one's path of learning.

As for me, I was still chafing under Ethel's disapproving eye and her continued rejections of any efforts I had made to care for her since the last incident. During a rare lucid moment one day, she had actually ordered me out of her room and demanded that someone else be assigned to her care.

"Why is she still so angry with me?" I asked.

"Deborah, it is hard for you to understand this right now, but no matter how wonderful our medicine is and how adept we have become at saving lives, not everyone wants to be resuscitated," Dolly responded. "Ethel is one of those people. She's behaving like a lot of people who get a chance to see the other side. If they get yanked back to this world, they're very angry for a long time. Ethel was crossing over to the other side. You pulled her back. She's angry with you for pulling her back. It's a natural response. Time will take care of this matter—for both of you. Here come Rose and Nancy. Let's get ready. Ethel really needs this prayer circle ceremony."

For the next half hour, the four of us stood in a circle around Ethel's bed and held the sacred prayer circle ceremony. These had become commonplace for us after Aunt Mel's stay on the unit. By this time I had participated in many such ceremonies and had observed how a number of other elderly patients had profited from them. I knew that Ethel could benefit from all the sources of support we could muster, spiritual as well as worldly.

None of us wanted to send her up for the ECT treatment, but that was not our choice.

Dolly, Rose, Nancy, and I lifted Ethel's frail body onto the gurney. As I headed out with her, I was feeling uneasy about the tenuous nature of her condition and the ambiguities of the situation.

It had now been more than a year and a half since my journey into the realm of the spirits had begun. I had almost completed the requirements for a second master's degree, this one in psychology, and I had completed the Kübler-Ross bereavement training. I felt myself being torn between the new experiences in the spiritual dimension and the demands of the medical science that had been my world for some twenty years. As I progressed on both tracks it seemed I was growing less sure of the importance of one over the other.

Ethel V. was securely strapped onto the gurney for her short trip to the second-floor treatment room where her ECT would be administered.

I had pushed her only a short distance down the hall when I caught the whiff of a distinctive and familiar odor. It was one I had come to know from my years of working around patients who were nearing the end of life. My medical peers and I knew it as the smell of death. Suddenly, it frightened me again.

As I pushed the gurney past the nurse's station, the smell seemed to intensify. I looked around to locate the source. I paused and looked into one of the patient rooms to see if it might be coming from there. No one was in the room. I tried to dismiss the notion that something was wrong.

I looked at my watch. It was already a few minutes past the appointment for delivering Ethel to the treatment room, so I put the smell out of my mind. I told myself it was my imagination, which had been on quite a spree anyway. But the odor did not go away.

As I unlocked the double doors leading out of the unit and pushed the gurney into the hallway where the elevators were located, the odor was still present. I became uncomfortable and apprehensive. The odor's metallic quality seemed to add a chill to the air. I shivered as I turned to relock the double doors behind me.

As I turned back to my charge on the gurney, I caught sight of a large, opaque figure in front of me. It filled the space between the top of the gurney on which Ethel was strapped and the wall to my left. I stared in disbelief at a figure with all the physical characteristics of the winged angels I had seen in books.

This apparition isn't like any of the others I have seen, I thought to myself. It was larger and more distinct in form. I was frozen in place with my hands firmly on the gurney. I looked down at Ethel, to make sure she was okay. The rhythmic rise and fall of the crisp white sheet that covered her body told me she was alive and fast asleep.

My eyes swept the length of the image hovering in front of me. I sensed the entity was an angel, a type of transition angel whose assignment was to help human souls with their journey to the afterlife. If there was any earthly reason for me to be able even to see this particular angel at all, it had to be because of my interference with the departure of the old woman's spirit when her relatives had come for her earlier. I can only surmise that I had not fully learned my lesson about "letting go" at that point, because in the blink of an eye, I panicked. I was still not willing to let anyone or any thing, not even a transition angel from the other side, take

Ethel. I bolted out of the alcove with Ethel's gurney in tow, down the hall toward the elevators.

The entire episode took only seconds but seemed to last an eternity.

As I waited anxiously for the elevator doors to open, I looked back to see if the figure was still there. I could see all the way down to the alcove and the door. There was nothing. The figure was gone.

Once I was sure that everything had returned to normal, my next concern was for Ethel's condition. I clumsily took her thin wrist to feel for a pulse. My own pounding heartbeat interfered with my ability to detect hers, so I checked the movement of the sheet over her chest. It was still moving up and down in a slow, even pattern. I felt relieved that she had slept through the whole thing.

I delivered Ethel V. to the treatment room and, without comment, turned her over to the two physicians waiting for her.

I went immediately back downstairs and straight to the medicine room. I closed the door behind me and leaned against the wall, sobbing. The episode had left me more rattled and drained than any of the preceding ones. By now I should have been accustomed to seeing apparitions. But this experience was having a much greater impact on me than any of the others. It was one thing to see apparitions of family members coming for a loved one. It was something completely different to see an angel, like the ones depicted in religious books and paintings, coming for a person. Did it come for Ethel's soul, or had it been sent from the spirit world to force me to come to terms with my fear of letting go?

Dolly entered the medicine room and found me in the corner,

crying like a baby. After giving her a cursory report of my experience with Ethel and the angel, I begged to be left alone. Understanding the magnitude of what had happened, she agreed to watch my patients for the balance of the afternoon. Nancy would retrieve Ethel from upstairs.

Then for the first time in my career, I left work before my shift was over. I drove to the pond at the edge of the Plantation's property and sat in my car, staring at the trees. The colors seemed brighter; the scenery seemed rearranged or different somehow from the many times I had studied it before. One thought kept playing over and over again as I tried to blot out the images of that day: *My actions will cost me something.*

My meddling at this point in Ethel's transition would not be without consequences for me. I knew the actions I had taken to resuscitate her and to tear her away from the transition angel had seriously interrupted the progress of my shamanic training. It would not take long to learn the nature of those consequences.

I was late for work the next morning after my experience with Ethel and the angel. The night had passed slowly, because I woke frequently from dreams that seemed all too real.

Because I showed up late and had left early without explanation the previous day, my coworkers met me at the door with worry lines etched on their faces. Even Dolly looked concerned.

"What's going on, Deborah?" Dolly was her usual assertive self and demanded answers for the trio.

When I didn't answer right away, she said, "We've taken care of things on the unit for the time being." She gave me a follow-me wave, and we all trooped into the pharmacy room.

She shut the door behind us.

I quickly told the three women the entire story of what had happened in the alcove outside the unit the day before. My bizarre tale tumbled out in a steady stream of words. I described the apparition I had seen without interruption.

When I stopped to catch my breath, Dolly chuckled. "That visitor was here for a reason all right." She said it matter-of-factly, with a knowing nod. The things I was describing were shocking to me, but they did not seem to faze Dolly in the least. "You did not let Ethel's ancestors have her. Okay—so they sent a stronger messenger."

Although she was acting blasé about the whole thing, I still had the impression she was more interested in this phenomenon than in any of my previous encounters with the spirit world. Rose and Nancy both stared, wide-eyed, at my description of the angelic image.

"What did it look like? Did it say anything to you? What happened next?"

I was forced to go over my story several times. Still, their questions continued.

I had the strange feeling that something had happened to me that had never happened to any of them. Even so, Dolly maintained her air of authority.

"I interfered once, Deborah, when I stepped between what I thought was a night nurse and a dying patient. Remember I told you about it several months ago? Later that night a transition angel came for that woman anyway." Dolly had finally revealed the ending to one of her own stories about seeing apparitions around her patients.

"We all, ultimately, in one way or another, have to come to terms with the inevitable. We must all enter the spirit world. It just depends on how we do it and who our escorts will be," she said.

We had discussed what the shaman women called the "afterlife" on many occasions, before my experiences with Ethel V. The women contended that many of our elderly patients, especially those with advanced forms of Alzheimer's and other senile dementias, were in the final preparation phase for having their human soul move into the spirit world. That's why there was so much spirit activity on this unit, they would tell me over and over.

All three women concurred that the emanations we observed at the Plantation were visitations from the spirit world by spirit elders. "It's the spirit elders who are talking to us many times when we're working with our patients," Rose finally admitted.

"There are spirit elders, and then there are other types of spirits," Dolly said. "The elders are the wise ones that should be listened to." The women claimed to know the difference.

"You must learn to differentiate the messages you receive as well as the messengers who deliver them," Dolly often told the little group. "You must learn to decipher whether they are coming from the spirit elders or from trickster spirits, who are trying to mislead you and send you off in another direction."

I was so new on the path to this dimension that I could not begin to differentiate one type of spirit from another. Until my experiences with Ethel, I could barely accept the reality of what I was seeing or sensing, let alone decode the traveling papers of the spirits I encountered.

My own lack of knowledge was the main reason I wanted one of the shaman women to verify or explain to me what I had seen with each spirit or apparition encounter. It was not to be. Instead, I continued to be led along a path that was guided by what Dolly called the biggest roadblock to my progress—my fear of letting go, my inability to come to terms with death.

Thus came the first toll I would have to pay for my meddling.

"Deborah, I have watched you these past months and recognized the internal struggles you have about death. I understand the origins of those struggles," Dolly said. "I have talked to the spirit elders about it often. We understand your conflicts in this area contribute to your having a hard time working with these old people, especially the demented ones. Letting any of them go into the other world causes you great difficulty."

A numbness set in as I listened to this woman. Her words cut like a knife to the very core of my soul.

"You are beating up on yourself for not being able to overcome these struggles. It is playing out in your work with these old people," she said. "You are only compounding your agony as a result. Deborah, you are no different than anyone else who works with these demented people. The work gets to all of us until we understand what is really happening. Working with these patients is hard— hearing the same questions over and over, dealing with the erratic behaviors, watching the aimless wandering, knowing what some of them used to be like in better days. And then thinking that the ultimate outcome for all of your efforts will still be the patient's death. It takes a lot to work with these people. We all run out of stamina. Sometimes even *I* want to scream."

I had never heard Dolly acknowledge that the work here stressed her as well as the other two women. They always seemed so even-tempered, so cool and cheerful with these old people.

"Deborah, your enemy—the obstacle that keeps blocking your progress on this spiritual journey—is letting go," Dolly said, her eyes never leaving mine. "Death is not the enemy you seem to think it is. Your real enemies are the things in your life that cause you to feel fear and hate. They produce an anger in you which interferes with your ability to reach out to these people. That anger, in turn, drains your spirit of any joy that could be derived from this experience."

How did anger get into the picture? I wondered to myself. *I thought my problem was letting go.*

"Hey, I give these old people the best care I can." I was getting defensive. Her words began swirling around in my head. Suddenly I felt caught up in a cyclone of images, emotions, and memories of days gone by.

The stout Native American nurse had never let on that she, too, was troubled by many of the same things that exhausted me. In the midst of the swirling images in my head, I thought about what she was saying. She was right, as usual. I had been complaining more. I was tired of the constant noise and some of the more demented patients we had at the time. There was a lot of tension on the unit. I would often complain about wanting to get away from the Plantation and work somewhere else. But circumstances were such that I could not do that. Some of the patients' families were irritating me, particularly Ethel's two nieces.

"You must make friends with these enemies of yours," Dolly

said as she continued this particular lesson. "You must identify the source—each person, place, or situation that precipitates this anger in you. As long as a person, place, or situation can evoke anger, or frustration, or fear in you, it holds all of the power. You have allowed it to have power over you and your life."

I was exhausted from the events of the past twenty-four hours. A lesson about embracing my enemies was the last thing I wanted to hear. I wanted to scream "bullshit" at my shaman coworkers.

Instead, I bit my tongue and asked, "How can you make friends with an enemy—any enemy—that causes such strong feelings as anger and hate?"

"It is one of the most difficult things you will have to achieve on your journey," Dolly answered. "But you must take those steps if you ever hope to have your head and your heart truly connected. You have made much progress so far. This last episode with the transition angel tells me you have a way yet to go. It shows both progress and the presence of a stumbling block you are almost ready to overcome."

With that statement, Dolly and I left the others and went to Ethel's room. Once we assured ourselves that she was sleeping, Dolly resumed the lesson she had begun.

"First you must identify the source of a negative influence," she told me. "Next you must break it down into smaller parts. Then you can begin to come to terms with it."

My two years at the Plantation had become very stressful, very draining on me. I was feeling overwhelmed.

Dolly explained how to deal with that. I was to take an honest inventory of the positive and negative aspects of my job.

"Break it down," she said. "Ask yourself questions: Is it an individual patient or family member that is driving me up the wall? Or the incessant pacing, the repetitious drone of the la-la-la sounds many of the patients make? Is it the screamer, the person who will do nothing but scream for hours, disrupting the patients and driving the staff to near madness?"

"It's all of those—and more!" I said, laughing.

"Yes, but you can't deal with 'all of those,' " she said. "That's why you feel overwhelmed. You have to break those things down further into pieces you can manage. Even in the process of identifying the pieces of your troubles, you will find that you are starting to feel better. When you name them, you know them. They are finite. They have a beginning and an end. You can deal with them."

Dolly paused just long enough to see if I was staying with her, and I nodded.

"Okay, so you've gotten them broken down," she continued. "Then you can focus on each individual element. Don't think about what is bothering you. Think about what you can do to change it. If there is nothing you can do but wait it out, focus on how soon it will pass."

She talked about identifying the positive parts of every negative situation, shifting the focus toward those positive pieces that were within my ability to control or change. If I could not effect change, I should break down the problem into even smaller pieces that I could either intellectually accept or somehow manage with my own attitude.

"If you can do this," she said, "you will have developed the ability to make friends with the enemy that is making your life so miserable. Once that happens, it loses its power over you and its control, and then it slips away."

The whole idea was to shift my focus on the problem, shift my view of it, and then the power base would shift too. The ultimate, underlying goal of making friends with an enemy was to deprive the negative elements from having power over your life. When you do that, your soul takes control of the power.

It was a shaman's approach to power—to regaining power or acquiring power, shifting or protecting the power base. Dolly said it is on that level that the shaman works. Spiritual power in the world of the shaman is a viable entity. You don't have to see it to know that it works.

"It's like electricity," Dolly explained. "Electricity is a form of power. We can't see it. But we know it's there, and we can channel the end result and use it to make things happen. Power to the shaman is the same thing. It is a tool that can be used for many purposes."

Dolly was trying to give me the secret to the extraordinary abilities she, Rose, and Nancy had for handling even the worst of the patients on the unit. They were trying to show me a different way of viewing these old people and their debilitating conditions. I needed to understand each piece of my own negative reactions, my fears and frustrations about working with people who were so close to the end of life. Dolly said I had to take back my power so I could experience the joy of working with these very special patients, elderly patients who possessed flourishing spirits.

"This is an important lesson," I said. "But what does it have to do with my problem of letting go?"

"What you did in pulling Ethel back, you did out of selfishness and guilt. Death holds power over you through your own fears and guilt," Dolly replied. "You must make friends with this enemy of yours, death. If you don't, its power over you will keep you locked away in fear of its presence for the rest of your life. You will not be able to move any further on your path."

Making friends with death would not be easy. It would take more than a single lesson about the topic for me to recognize that the essence of that internal shift in my soul had already taken place.

Following this lesson, Dolly and I returned to our regular duties. I was extra careful during the preparation of morning medicines, because I was still somewhat distracted by the events of the preceding day and the lesson Dolly had just given me.

All of the conversations about death and dying I had shared with my shaman friends were also whirling about in my brain as I went through the rote motions of that day. Intermingled with their words were the lessons I had learned in the Kübler-Ross workshops.

The dichotomy between my Western psychology studies and the shaman's spirit world was troubling. However, much of what I had learned from my shaman teachers, and even from Dr. Kübler-Ross, was confirmed for me through the inexplicable experiences I was having on the unit.

The existence of a spiritual dimension and the idea that death is simply a process of transitioning from this world to the next one in the afterlife were no longer philosophical or abstract concepts. By now I had been through too many up-close and personal contacts with apparitions to justify my continued skepticism. I still did not have the answers, but I had the "eyewitness" proof that there was— there is—another dimension in these old people's lives, even if I did not yet fully understand it.

Western medicine has difficulty even in talking about an afterlife, because it is impossible to quantify. I was no different. My acceptance was challenged by this inability to quantify the stories I was being told by Dolly and Rose. For me it took the Kübler-Ross workshops on death and dying to open my mind. I had to hear other people who, in my opinion, had more credibility and who had a language that allowed them to communicate similar concepts in such a way that they made sense to me. This allowed me to accept the things I was being told by my shaman coworkers more readily.

Now I had seen, or sensed, with my own faculties the phenomenal world of spirits and all that could be found within its expansiveness. This education of my faculties took time. Was this the "time" that Dolly had mentioned earlier when we talked before about my continued need to resuscitate Ethel? Was this the same "time" that Elisabeth Kübler-Ross mentioned in her workshops? In her many years of research into death and dying, she discovered that the "closer one gets to death, the more quickly the person's spiritual dimension of life expands and the more open that person is to spiritual events in life."

This is one explanation for why there were so many spirit manifestations, at such frequent intervals, at the Plantation. Nearly all of our patients were very close to dying, from years of failing health, from senile dementias like Alzheimer's, or simply from the wear and tear of living so long. If Kübler-Ross's research was correct, my shaman friends and I were working with a plethora of open doorways into the spiritual dimension.

As confusing as all of this information was, my experiences with Ethel V. were beginning to make some sense. I was no longer afraid to acknowledge my intuitive abilities. With the support of Dolly, Rose, and Nancy and this unit of elderly patients, I had a system, an environment, a structure that allowed me to go freely in and out of that sixth dimension.

I felt a new confidence that I could experience that dimension and still function in a concrete day-to-day, linear existence. With proper instruction and time, and working through my own doubts and fears, I was able to achieve some sense of balance. Having had these experiences and survived them, and returned to the humdrum of daily existence, I no longer felt so terribly confused or frightened. Death may not ever become my friend, as Dolly would have me believe, but I was at least beginning to come to terms with it.

Eventually I was able to figure out the meaning of the powerful, soul-wrenching experience that followed Ethel's resuscitation. After the episode with the transition angel, I finally understood the lesson about letting old people go when it's their time. It was unfortunate that Ethel V. had already been discharged before I was able to fit those pieces together.

After Ethel's final ECT treatment, her nieces came to get her. They informed us that they had decided to send her to one of the state-operated, long-term care facilities, because the nursing home where she had been housed was just too expensive. I doubted she had many days left, especially under the not-so-tender care of her two nieces.

But I knew she had a happy secret. It didn't really matter where she went after her stay at the Plantation. She was soon going to see some old relatives who really cared about her. My experiences with Ethel V. taught me that she and others like her are only "in transition" when they reach this late stage of dementia.

Carry Me Home

IT WAS NOW August 1991, and I was nearing my two-year anniversary of working with the staff at the Plantation.

Ethel V. had been gone from the unit for just over a week when I was assigned to a tiny eighty-year-old mountain woman from the Appalachian area not far from where I grew up. End-stage Alzheimer's disease had left this four-foot-eleven matron of a mountain clan deaf and mute, and completely unaware of her surroundings.

Her name was Ada, but all the members of the extended family who brought her to the neuro-psych unit called her Grannie. Two of her daughters and a brood of children—I don't know if the little ones were grandchildren or great-grandchildren—made the journey out of the mountains to bring Ada to the Plantation. Grannie was unable to walk, but the family did not own a wheelchair. She weighed only seventy-five or eighty pounds, and was carried onto the unit in the arms of a sullen young man, whom I assumed was also a relative. The family left soon after seeing that she had been settled into her room.

Ada wasn't emaciated and didn't have the gaunt appearance of many of my elderly female patients. She was simply a tiny woman to begin with, and I soon found that I could easily lift her from the bed to a wheelchair myself.

She arrived dressed in a thin washed-out nightgown and robe. The young women who brought her in to the hospital wore polyester slacks and flowered blouses—old clothes, but clean and pressed. One of the women carried Grannie's entire wardrobe of nightgowns and slippers with her in a brown-paper shopping bag.

The visual image of this clan of mountain folks was chaotic. Each time they came to visit, it was like a colorful scene from an episode of the *Beverly Hillbillies*.

The relatives who visited seemed most concerned that Grannie Ada did not talk to them. They thought she was angry with the whole family. No one in the family was able to grasp the medical explanation for her condition. Although they were told repeatedly that it was the result of an advanced stage of Alzheimer's, which had robbed her of any ability to communicate, it meant little to them. They simply wanted her "fixed" so they could "get their Grannie Ada back." They didn't understand the impossibility of that request.

Medicare was paying for her stay, which meant she wouldn't be at the Plantation very long. We had a maximum thirty-day window to do everything that needed to be done.

Our primary purpose was to get as definitive a diagnosis as possible. Her relatives were intimidated by the hospital surroundings and reluctant to talk. They answered only the questions they were asked and didn't volunteer additional information.

They had brought Grannie Ada down because their family physician in the mountains had told them that the doctors at our facility would be able to help her. They had no idea what was wrong with her.

"She won't talk to us," one of Ada's daughters said. "We tried everything we could to get her to talk. She just sits in her chair on the porch and stares out at the woods. We don't know why she's so mad at us. She's been that way for a long, long time."

Now they were in this big-city, high-tech environment with a bunch of "high-falutin' " doctors. They were under the impression that the doctors here would give her some medicine. Then she would be okay. She'd start talking again and everything would be back to the way it was before.

Grannie Ada was the matriarch of this very large family, earning her status by outliving everybody and having a bushel of kids, who'd had kids of their own.

We put her through the standard diagnostic workup she had come for. We drew blood, catheterized her to get a urine sample, gave her a CT scan and EKG—the basic diagnostic evaluation procedures to gather data on her condition.

Once that process was finished and we were waiting for the information to come back, I could spend longer uninterrupted periods with her—often as much as an hour at a time. I had to feed and bathe her. Sometimes it would take forty-five minutes just to feed her. Because she had a very advanced form of Alzheimer's, she was losing the ability to swallow. I would give her half a spoonful of food and wait as she worked it around in her mouth before she was able to swallow it. She took liquids through a straw, but even then I had to coax her.

Ada was such a dear little woman that these extra chores did not seem like chores at all. Ironically, by some twist of fate, she had ended up in our most luxurious private room. It was a quiet room, out of the main traffic flow of the unit, with two corner windows. The windows opened up to trees on one side and blue skies on the other. I chatted about the scenery. It was pretty, I said, but not as beautiful as the mountains we called home.

Rays of sunlight flooded the room at different times of the day, sometimes casting a rainbow of light on the opposite wall. I talked to Ada in a steady stream of conversation about everything going on around her—her tests, the relatives who had just left, the weather—whatever came to mind.

I do not recall the exact moment I realized she was trying to communicate with me too. I had just picked her up out of the bed and put her into a wheelchair. A glow appeared around her, and I thought for a moment it was the rainbow effect of the sunlight touching her hair.

Slowly an intuitive conversation began to take place. I could feel her communicating with me, although there was no sound. I was surprised but not shocked. It came in just like a regular conversation would start between two people. Yet, when I thought about it later, I couldn't put it into words. It was like the conversations you have in a dream, when, after waking, it is the feeling and not the words you recall. I felt that Ada had a request of me, but then the moment passed.

After that episode, I tried to spend more time with her, whenever my schedule permitted. Ada was not a sophisticated person, like my treasured friend Aunt Mel. But she was a wise old woman and I enjoyed her company.

After experiencing the same thing several more times, I felt comfortable with this new method of intuitive communication.

Eventually I felt I could completely understand everything Ada was telling me without hearing her say a single word.

As the days passed, I began to get a sense of great urgency in Ada and what she was trying to tell me. Ada was tired of living. She was ready to cross over to the other side. Folks from that part of the mountains, I know from experience, are tuned in to spirits and ghosts and angels coming to carry them home. Soon these were the images filling our conversations.

Ada wanted to be with her other family members who had passed on from their mountain valley in generations before.

She believed she had done her duties for the family. But the children, grandchildren, and great-grandchildren were holding on to her and didn't want to let her go. Everyone expected her to get well, to come back home and be the matriarch of the clan again.

I began these conversations talking aloud to her, then moved to an intuitive level of conversation. I sometimes responded to her verbally from habit. But she never spoke, ever. Not a word.

Her eyes were at play during our conversations, and although she was mute, I could have sworn she became more fully alert physically when we were engaged in these talks.

It was no longer disconcerting for me to encounter the spirits of my elderly demented patients. From the first time I saw the glow of Ada's spirit and listened to its soft, reasoning message, it was clear to me I was being confronted by an almost pure, unadulterated form of life.

Almost every human aspect of Ada had now passed on, and she was just lingering in the withering shell of the body. It filled me with awe to realize I was in the presence of a full-blown spirit, an evolving angel as I liked to call her. Ada's body was fading and barely there, but her spirit was vivid. The body was ravaged, but the soul was so complete.

All of my twenty-plus years of experience with death and dying seemed to be coming into focus with this experience. The whole question about what happens to the human life force—one day or moment you see and talk to someone alive, the next day or minute they are dead—was now answered for me. A lifetime burden seemed to be lifting. Everything is so natural! The life force, that energy—which some call "the spirit" or the "soul"—leaves the body to continue on to another, indefinable experience. It was also clear to me that this end-of-life-transition is a journey the spirit wants to make, is prepared for, and looks forward to taking.

Despite the pragmatism of my worldly, medical science training—a technological expertise I still value highly—I was now more comfortable with operating in two different, perhaps "parallel" worlds. I found no ambiguity in doing so; in fact, in my experience the worlds of science and the spirit can be complementary. Perhaps for some, the two worlds are incompatible, and if a person cannot make the necessary leap of faith between science and shamanism, it can be dangerous. The experience can be confusing, even maddening at times. But like my Native American friends, I accepted that there is more to life than this rag, and bone, and hank of hair.

Of course, I could not explain away everything in the spirit world, any more that our most brilliant physicists and geneticists can explain away everything in their hard sciences. And, like my Native American mentors, I would never try. I only knew for certain that Ada's spirit had found a way to make her wishes known.

And I knew I had to be very, very careful how I dealt with the adult members of her family.

Early in my nursing training I had served a public health rotation in the foothills of the Smoky Mountains. That experience gave me insight into the lives of these mountain people.

I could almost envision this family's cluster of mountain shacks, with several generations living together in and around the same area all their lives. The family members would live in the same "holler" or one or two "ridges" over. They were very clannish and probably used a lot of what we'd call home remedies. I cannot swear to it, but I would not have been surprised if they were moonshiners.

Ada's female relatives brought the young kids along for every visit—some of the children were only three or fours years old. But there was seldom an adult male in the group. After every visit, they made the long drive home because the women had to cook supper for the rest of the family. The unspoken truth was they didn't have enough money to rent a hotel room and stay in town.

This clannish isolation caused them to be distrustful of anyone from outside their own families. Ada acknowledged that I might have trouble getting through to them. She knew the younger women thought she was angry with them. This frustrated her. She said she was not angry with anyone and did not ignore their questions on purpose. Ada did suggest that if any of her kin had something on their minds to tell her—one last time, to make peace with her— that would be fine. She implored me to speak for her.

I assured Ada that I would speak to the daughters and grand-daughters on her behalf, and do my best to convince them of how things were with her.

On the next visit, the small children, unlike their mothers, were no longer in awe of the sterile shining walls of the Plantation. They had been here before and found nothing threatening. They became especially unruly—little wild and free creatures of the mountains undaunted even by these strange walls. Like young river otters in joyous play, they tumbled, darted, and tripped over one another behind the chairs where their elders were seated. The boys were pinching and teasing the girls, who in turn bumped and shoved them back, then skittered away.

I could see their lives, free of constraint in the moss-covered hills, and I could clearly see the mixtures of the colors of rich brown earth and red clay worn into the dusty knees and elbows of their shirts and pants. They obviously had been rolling around in the yard in what was probably their Sunday-best attire before being forced to come down the mountain for this visit. Children like these, I knew from those home visits I had made as a student nurse, were only slightly tamed by changing civilization. They came into the house just long enough to eat and sleep before going back outside where they could run free in the woods again.

Theirs was a childhood of freedom not unlike my own in the foothills, just a few dozen ridges and hollers north of the mountains where these children played. They were wilder and freer, only because they lived higher and farther back in the mountains.

I knew I could not tell the women the things Grannie Ada wanted me to tell them as long as the children were romping in the small room. So, soon after we all settled around Ada, I called Nancy to come take these wild little creatures out into the garden while I conducted some serious business. Ada's business.

After the children had been safely corraled out of the room, the two women, who were in their late thirties, eased themselves back in their chairs. I had taken Grannie from her bed and strapped her into a wheelchair so she could be on a level playing field for her visit with these family members. She sat facing the two women and I stood behind her.

The women immediately began inquiring about their Grannie's prognosis. I told them they would have to talk to her doctors, that I was not authorized to discuss her medical condition. However, I did tell them that Ada had only a short time left with the family, that she had reached a point in her condition, in her Alzheimer's, when all of her bodily functions were slowly shutting down. I told them her thinking abilities, as well as her abilities to speak and hear, were already gone. That was why she no longer spoke to them. I assured them she was not angry with anyone.

"How long does she have?" one of the women asked.

"It could be weeks," I said, "maybe a few months."

All day I had worried about what I would say, could say, to these family members. I certainly could not tell them that Ada had asked me to speak to them on her behalf. They would have immediately wanted to know how I had learned that from her. They had already been informed by the doctors that she could not speak to them, but I still sensed they did not fully believe it. To now claim that I had communicated with their old Grannie would have only reinforced their belief that she was truly mad at them and purposely not talking.

So I explained why her mute condition was only part of her illness. I explained that like cobwebs, the Alzheimer's disease had spread through her brain and shut off her abilities to speak and to think and react to them.

They understood the concept of cobwebs. One of the women said, "Oh, so it's them cobwebs that's coverin' her brain that's keepin' her from hearin' us and talkin' to us?"

"Yes," I replied. Communicating with these women in a language they could understand was very important for everyone involved. If that required using analogies to nature, then so be it.

I went on to tell them that the same disease was now making it impossible for her automatic functions, such as swallowing food and water, to continue without outside assistance. I said that eventually some other physical event such as a heart attack or pneumonia, or an infection of some kind would put an end to her life.

They seemed to understand. Then I took a deep breath and stepped across the line into the domain of the spirit world.

"Your Grannie Ada is going to pass on soon," I said with some trepidation. "But right now, although she can't speak or let you know that she recognizes any of you, her spirit is still alive and active.

"In a few days we will have done everything we can do here. Someone will call and tell you to come pick up Ada and take her home. When you get her back home, tell everyone in the family who wants to talk to her to come visit. Anyone who has unfinished business with her should come to her house and tell her whatever still needs to be said. Her spirit is very much alive inside her. Her spirit can hear and will take these last messages across with her."

The women were staring at Ada in a new way, as if they were reassessing her capacity to be with them. Their expressions were almost quizzical, as if they had happened upon a burning bush in the hills that spoke to them. The tiny little bundle of humanity in the chair in front of me just sat very still and silent.

"Can her spirit hear us talking right now?" the younger of the two women asked.

I nodded. "Yes."

I am sure most doctors would have been horrified by my answer, but my own strange experiences up to that point made me confident that Ada had indeed been an eager eavesdropper on this conversation.

"You go back home now, and tell everybody who has unfinished business to take care of with Ada to come and tell her about it. Don't expect her to show any sign of response, but tell them that she can hear them. Tell her you love her. Tell her you're sorry if you've done something that needs fixing. But come and tell her good-bye, because your Grannie is preparing to cross over. Her spirit will hear your words and know their meaning."

The women nodded.

I had a clear picture in my mind of Ada's little wooden house, sitting in some hollow or on a ridge surrounded by several other houses of her clan. There would be many relatives, children—some already very old themselves—grandchildren, great-grandchildren, nieces, cousins, aunts, and uncles—generations all living close by, just as they had for two hundred years. Many, many would come, waiting in lines on the low porch for their turn to enter the dimly lit room where Ada would be waiting for them to come and make their peace.

These two women understood spirits, and could accept that they no longer needed to hang on to Grannie Ada. It was all right to let her go; she was not mad at them, only very old and very sick and tired. There was a look of relief on the women's faces as they kissed Ada good-bye and fussed over her in the hospital one last time.

They said they would be back to fetch her as soon as the doctors told them she could go home. They called the little ones in, restraining their tumbling play long enough to kiss their Grannie.

Several days later the women came for Ada. I told Dolly I wanted to see the old woman all the way out to the car. I carefully eased her into the wheelchair and straightened her nightgown and the threadbare robe she had been wearing when she arrived. She told me good-bye and thanked me for getting her message to her kinfolk.

I pushed her wheelchair to the elevator, past the spot where the transition angel had appeared before Ethel and me only a few weeks before. This time I felt some sense of peace about letting this old woman go.

A vintage, rusting station wagon was waiting at the curb in front of the Plantation. Thick red clay and dust from the mountain roads around Ada's home concealed the color of the old Buick, if any paint was left at all.

I tucked Ada's shriveled little body into the ragged, patched backseat, and she sank down with the sagging springs. When the door closed, only a wisp of her white hair was visible above the window edge.

The ever-present children shouted with glee because Grannie was out of the hospital. They scrambled over the seat from the wagon's rear compartment, legs flailing, bare feet in the air, pushing and shoving to be the one to sit next to her.

The young women collecting her told me word had spread across the holler that Grannie was coming home. Everyone was waiting to see the old woman. Relatives were coming from all over the hills to pay their respects and settle up accounts with their matriarch.

I watched the car drive away, pouring out an exhaust of blue-gray smoke—Ada's chariot departing into the clouds to take her home.

The old woman's circle of life was almost complete. I searched my mind for the familiar foreboding, the sense of dread that someone's death was near, that I would be forced to let go. And I found only joy in my heart.

The next several weeks passed quickly. I had apparently finished my lessons about the spirit world because I had no more encounters with spirits.

It was now the autumn of 1991, and time for me to move on. My academic course work was nearly completed and my clinical training was about to begin. I would not be able to continue working at the Plantation. When I announced my departure date, my fellow nurses congratulated me on my progress, both in my academic pursuits and in my shamanic training. Dolly, Rose, and Nancy said they had taken me as far down the shaman's pathway as their spirit elders would allow them to go with me.

"Sister, that block between your head and your heart is gone," Dolly said. "You can see into our world now, the world of the spirits. Before you leave we must have a small ceremony to celebrate."

For my last afternoon on the unit, the patients were unusually quiet, as if the spirits themselves had decided to give us this space. Dolly, Rose, Nancy, and I sat together in a ceremonial circle in the nurse's lounge. As part of the ceremony they asked me to review with them the events at the Plantation that had propelled me along my shamanic journey, up to this point of my impending departure. I surmised that it was a shamanic version of pregraduation orals.

For nearly an hour I talked to them about the different lessons this symphony of earthbound spirits had taught me. Momma Sissy taught me to hear spirits through music. Sara's spirit showed me how important it is to be surrounded by a loving family at the end of one's life. Ruthie's lesson was about the good and bad days that can come toward the end. One must learn to go with the flow, enjoy the good days, and ride out the bad ones. Aunt Mel's dramatic appearance on the unit drove home for me the impact that loneliness and isolation can have on an old person's spirit. Stephen and Barbara Z.'s golden threads showed me what holds people together who love each other as much as they did. Last but not least, the hardest lessons for me were about letting go of another person's spirit and understanding that transition angels come to help the spirit cross over into the afterlife. It took the spirits of both Ethel and Grannie Ada to show me that lesson.

"Very good, Deborah," Rose said. "Did these elders teach you anything else?"

"Yes," I replied. "There is little honor in growing old these days, not like there once was. That's unfortunate, because these old people and their spirits have made one thing very clear to me. Old people really are unrecognized treasures—even the ones with dementia. They all have a special kind of wisdom that comes only from living life, through the good times and the bad. No monetary value can ever be placed on that."

I looked to my three mentors for approval and then continued. "Another important lesson I learned from these patients and their families centered on relationships with other people. Relationships with others are the most important things a person can have in life. They are the buffers for the rough times and the good times that come in anyone's life, no matter what their age.

"The life lessons these old people taught me transcend the changing winds of time. The old, old people know this. That's part of what makes them so wise.

"People with Alzheimer's disease seem to recognize the importance of personal and family relationships more quickly than many of their peers. I am sure that is due in part to knowing that at some point they will have to rely on others for everything. Those with warm, loving relationships seem to have an easier time of it. Those who haven't cultivated such relationships have a much harder time. The old adage '*what goes around comes around*' really seems to play out with time doesn't it?"

The three women nodded their agreement.

"The demented patients, especially those with Alzheimer's, taught me a lesson that only they can. They are all evolving angels. Each one of them showed me how *the veil that separates the spirit world from ours grows thinner with age.* The more withered the person's physical body becomes, the stronger the spirit grows. As the end of this life approaches, visions of the other side get clearer and one's ability to talk to the spirits of loved ones on the other side gets easier. People who do not understand this phenomenon get upset and back away. For those who are willing to embrace it, the rewards can be great." ⌡

Once I had completed my review, the three women and I celebrated the event.

Concerned that my experiences with the spirit world would come to an end once I left my job at the Plantation, I posed one final question to my mentors. I asked if my encounters with the spirits were over.

They answered me in unison. "Your dance with the spirit world has just begun!"

I could not know it then, but these wise women, whom I am convinced were true shamans in the full sense of the Native American description, were seeing into my future with their predictions.

My journey over the next decade would take me through studies with other Native Americans in the western United States, to Australia for a meaningful experience with Aboriginal women in the Outback, and through a near-death experience of my own. On this ten-year journey I would spend considerable time delving into the spiritual dimensions of the circle of birth-life-death-rebirth. My future guides would be spirit sisters, like my mentors at the Plantation—Native American women who furthered my studies of the spirit world and Australian Aboriginal women who introduced me to studies of the dreamtime and jukurrpa.

The insights I gained in that sometimes strange, sometimes frightening, always wonderful period with my three shaman guides have helped me find a message of hope where there was only despair, a message of comfort where there was only pain.

For those patients and families confronting the challenges of a neurodegenerative disease and senile dementia, especially the Alzheimer's type, I can say one thing with confidence: There is a spiritual dimension that surrounds a demented elder. It grows with each passing day the disease is present. Indeed, if you are willing to look beyond the mask of any senile dementia, you will find unbounded beauty, serenity, and spiritual gratification.

Songs of Hope

NEARLY A DECADE has passed since I began working at
the Plantation. The twentieth century and the second millennium have come to an end. The third millennium is in its in-
fancy. The spirits of all but one of the people described in this book
have made their journey with the transition angel into the afterlife.
At last report Aunt Mel is alive and well and approaching her hun-
dreth birthday. If she reaches it, she will join a prestigious group of
centenarians. Membership in this exclusive club is growing. Cur-
rently it has more than 50,000 members in the United States. Authorities project that over the next forty years, its membership will
swell to more than a million people in just this country alone.

Some attribute Aunt Mel's longevity to genetics. Others suggest
that her involvement in the special programs offered at her assisted-
living residence has made a significant difference. One particular
program is a weekly Tai Chi class for seniors. As part of a national
eight-center research study on Tai Chi's effects on the prevalence

of falls among elder residents, Aunt Mel helped the investigators gather some rather remarkable data. She and the researchers were able to demonstrate that Tai Chi helped to improve her balance and mood and that of her peers. They also found that it reduced stress; lowered blood pressure; reversed fragility in the old, old; promoted faster recovery from heart attacks; and helped longevity. Quite a remarkable feat for a little old woman who was once thought to be demented and possessed by malevolent spirits!

In the last decade of the 1990s, other wonderful things have started to happen for the aging adults who followed after Momma Sissy, Ethel, Ada, and the others I met at the Plantation. Aging has become one of the most important topics in the world. In fact, it is so important that the United Nations declared 1999 as the International Year of Older Persons. They wanted to focus the world's attention on a unique occurrence taking place in the year 2000 when, for the first time in history, the elderly around the world would outnumber children. Recognizing this fact, members of the United Nations, the World Health Organization, the European Community, and the U.S. National Academy of Science joined forces to draft a set of eighteen priorities for improving the quality of life of elderly people around the world.

Authorities in America have noted that over the next thirty years, the number of people over the age of sixty-five will swell from 35 million to more than 80 million. The chronic illnesses that accompany the normal aging process are slowly beginning to take on a new degree of importance.

Spirituality, as a component of health, is only now being considered by traditional Western medical practitioners. They and scientists are beginning to admit that there is something more in the universe than what they can prove with their double-blind studies. No longer are medical pioneers like Elisabeth Kübler-Ross, M.D., Raymond Moody, M.D., and Melvin Morse, M.D. forced to labor alone in the quest for a better understanding of the spiritual dimensions in living and dying. Scientists and theologians are finding common ground in agreeing that there is more to humanity than flesh, blood, and bone—something my shaman coworkers and their tribal elders and ancestors have known for centuries.

In a few medical schools across the country, young student and resident physicians are being exposed to courses in how to deliver end-of-life care for the first time ever. In some of those programs, the concept of spirituality and the importance of a person's religious beliefs are stressed.

Such developments mark major milestones for Western medicine. In other countries, where the notion of the human spirit is more readily acknowledged, the spiritual dimension of healing is already an important part of healthcare.

Despite these many advances in traditional mainstream healthcare, the topic of spirituality and dementia is still in an embryonic stage. A few groups at select American academic centers and the National Institute on Aging are struggling with the issue of how to quantify spirituality in a dementia patient. Once they can establish just "what it is," they can develop research studies to prove its existence. Then they can go about measuring its impact on the demented person's quality of life.

I was exceedingly fortunate to have Dolly, Rose, and Nancy sharing some of their Native American and Afro-Caribbean ancestral knowledge about this topic with me—ten years ago. Now, the spiritual dimension for people with any form of senile dementia is as real to me as the air we breathe.

My experiences with those nurses, the patients described in this book, and the dozens of other demented patients who came to the Plantation during that two-year period between 1989 and 1991 propelled me to undertake a postgraduate fellowship in aging and Alzheimer's disease research in 1995. Thanks to my shaman friends, I had within my grasp a recognition that a spiritual dimension does exist within demented patients of all types and an understanding of its importance. I needed to expand my knowledge of the biological, psychological, and social dimensions of aging and the illnesses that are so common to it. After the fellowship, I made this area my life's work.

As the number of aging adults continues to increase, the prevalence of conditions that can produce dementia also, unfortunately, grows. The National Institute on Aging notes that at the end of the twenty-first century, half of all Americans over the age of eighty-five will suffer some form of dementia. If this trend continues, the primary causes of dementia will go on being Alzheimer's disease (60 to 70 percent), vascular (11 to 20 percent), and vascular plus Alzheimer's disease (1 to 20 percent), Parkinson's disease (8 percent), and head injuries (4 percent). Other less frequently occurring conditions that may contain some form of dementia in their clinical presentation will include Huntington's disease, Lewy Body disease, Pick's disease, Normal Pressure Hydrocephalus, Down syndrome, and AIDS.

With this in mind, organizations such as the Alzheimer's Association, the Ronald and Nancy Reagan Research Institute, the American Heart Association, and the American Parkinson's Association are stressing the urgent need for a new national emphasis on these diseases of aging.

"The treatment and strategies we have in place will not be sufficient to stem the rising tide of the number of elderly suffering from dementia," a Reagan Research Institute spokesman noted. "There must be a series of breakthroughs in treatment."

As research into the origins of these diseases progresses, new information about them is being revealed. And breakthroughs are being reported.

The National Institute on Aging and a number of medical research centers around the world are exploring methods for diagnosing dementia before memory loss even begins. Two American projects that show some promise are the use of computerized axial tomography (CT scan) and functional magnetic resonance imaging (MRI), along with neuropsychological testing. Other studies, which would develop tests for several different proteins in the blood and spinal fluid, have been suggested. Scientists at twenty-six Alzheimer's Disease Research Centers have already successfully identified a test for a genetic marker that is present in some forms of Alzheimer's disease.

While new and improved diagnostic measures are examined, ongoing research studies have unveiled new hope for the prevention and treatment of dementia-producing diseases like cerebral vascular accidents (strokes) and Alzheimer's disease.

A newly developed drug for the treatment of strokes, given within six hours after the symptoms start, has been found to substantially reduce the potential for permanent impairment. Some speculate that this second revolutionary drug for stroke treatment may "turn stroke therapy upside-down."

Medical researchers have conducted a number of studies on treatment approaches that impact the course of Alzheimer's disease. Research conducted by the National Institute on Aging and a leading academic medical center found that anti-inflammatory drugs such as ibuprofen "taken for as little as two years appear to reduce the risk of Alzheimer's." According to this group of researchers, acetaminophen and aspirin had no effect on reducing the risk of Alzheimer's.

A very important longitudinal study by twenty-three Alzheimer's Disease Research Centers looked at drugs that "slow the progression of Alzheimer's." The results of this comprehensive study demonstrated that a daily intake of vitamin E "may slow important symptoms of Alzheimer's by about seven months."

Studies on the use of hormone replacement therapy in aging women found that an intake of estrogen by perimenopausal women could reduce their risk of developing Alzheimer's by up to fifty percent.

Two of the most exciting studies reported at the end of the twentieth century offer some of the greatest hope for the future of Alzheimer's disease—for those who have it or who are at risk for developing it.

A joint American-Swedish study of postmortem brain tissue from five cancer patients demonstrated that cell growth occurs in human brains and that "human brains retain the potential for self-renewal throughout life." This remarkable study has led researchers to speculate that if they can find a way to stimulate brain cell regrowth, they may be able to treat such diseases as Alzheimer's and Parkinson's diseases.

In a separate study, American researchers reported the development of a vaccine which, in mice, appears to "ward off the brain-clogging deposits that are characteristic of Alzheimer's disease." The researchers also discovered that the vaccine "mopped up existing deposits " that were already present. While the vaccine appeared to be effective in mice, its impact on human brains with Alzheimer's disease remains to be seen. Medical researchers at this stage, though, are hopeful. They speculate that if studies of the vaccine's use in humans prove successful, determining who will benefit from its appropriate use will be the next step. One Canadian researcher suggested that this study raises the prospect of using immunization to treat or prevent other diseases that have comparable biological markers, such as Parkinson's disease, Creutzfeldt-Jakob disease, and myeloma.

With advances in understanding the origins of the diseases of aging will come methods for their effective treatment and prevention. By the middle of the twenty-first century it is possible that some of the neurodegenerative diseases, such as Alzheimer's, could be eradicated. This statement is based on the growing research into the identification of the different factors that separate those people who develop diseases from those who age successfully without developing any of them.

From a ten-year multisite study, medical researchers have already identified three key characteristics that contribute to successful aging: a low risk of disease development and disease-related disability, high mental and physical functioning, and an active engagement in life. Other factors which help to promote successful aging included such things as performing some type of daily exercise, resistance training with weights/weight-lifting, engaging in projects that keep a person intellectually stimulated, maintaining a strong social support system, volunteering for activities that are personally rewarding, eating a low-calorie diet, and adjusting one's attitude about aging. Additionally, those who believe they can have an influence on things that happen to them were found to fare better, both physically and mentally.

While physical, psychological, and social factors that contribute to successful aging have been identified, those within the spiritual domain that contribute to an elder's quality of life have not. Recent RAND Corporation studies show that a large percentage of the American population already knows about angels, believes in a spiritual dimension to the present world, and is convinced there is a life after an earthly death. Many come to these beliefs through religious teachings; many others are led to them by their own inexplicable life encounters.

Still, mainstream Western medicine, as a whole, balks at discussions about spirits and their inclusion in any part of the current healthcare system. While we have a long way to go in recognizing the spiritual dimensions of life, particularly in our elderly population of patients with dementia, modern healthcare practitioners have glimmers of hope. In the early 1990s, the National Institutes of Health funded a major new division for the exploration of complementary and alternative healing methods. Within that new division are categories of study, which include examples of practices "not commonly used, accepted, or available in conventional medicine." Under the section on mind-body medicine is a subcategory which is looking into the "relationship of religion and spirituality to biological function and several clinical conditions." Under a separate section on alternative medical systems is a subcategory on traditional indigenous systems such as Native American medicine, traditional Aboriginal medicine, Curanderismo, Ayurvedic medicine, and traditional African medicine.

It is my fervent hope that those who are exploring the connections between spirituality and dementia will come across people like Dolly, Rose, and Nancy, who can teach them about the intricacies of charting a path into the spirit world of an elderly person's life. This special group of women helped me to take my first small step on the path to recognizing and understanding the spiritual dimension and its magnificent presence among my demented patients those many years ago. I know there are others like them out there waiting to show the way. I encountered some of them after I left my job at the Plantation.

They all repeat the same message. The cycle of birth, life, death, and rebirth holds many mysteries and magic for everyone, scientists and shamans alike. Those who can quiet their minds and open their hearts will be able to hear the songs the spirits sing.

And just as my shaman friends predicted, my dance with the spirits goes on and on, as endless as the cycle of life itself.

About the Author

Dr. Deborah A. Forrest's graduate education and research and clinical work in the field of gerontology (the study of aging) bring unique credentials to the authorship of *Symphony of Spirits*.

In 1990, shortly after she returned to graduate school for a doctoral degree in clinical psychology, Dr. Forrest began an association with Dr. Elisabeth Kübler-Ross, the world-famous thanatologist and best-selling author. Eventually that association led to a dissertation research project with the last of Dr. Kübler-Ross's death and dying/grief resolution groups.

Dr. Forrest's bereavement research brought her face to face with elderly patients and patients dying of such diseases as AIDS and cancer. She also has intimate personal experience with the challenges of coming to terms with death and dying. That research project and the doctoral degree program were completed in 1995. Immediately afterward, she began a one-year postdoctoral fellowship in geriatric neuropsychiatry at the University of Kentucky's Alzheimer's Disease Research Center and Sanders-Brown Center on Aging.

Prior to obtaining her doctoral degree and completing the

fellowship in aging, Dr. Forrest had completed a diploma nursing-school program in Tennessee and a master's degree nursing program at Pennsylvania State University. During the years she was studying for her undergraduate degree at night, Dr. Forrest worked by day as an operating-room staff nurse and then as a departmental manager in an academic center in Atlanta.

After obtaining the graduate degree in nursing, Dr. Forrest returned home to the South and took a position as the youngest operating-room manager of a major academic medical center in the United States. Within a few years she was working as a nurse-consultant to several Fortune 100 medical-device companies.

Presently, Dr. Forrest, a clinical psychologist and registered nurse, conducts seminars and lectures on aging, bereavement, and spirituality, as well as coping strategies for the challenges inherent in growing old in a society that values youth.

Dr. Forrest has published extensively in professional and technical journals in various fields of medicine and health technology and has taught and lectured in her fields of specialization. She has been listed among the *Who's Who in Professional and Executive Women* since 1987.

About the Writer

Clint Richmond is a veteran freelance journalist and nonfiction book author. As a reporter for the *Dallas Times Herald*, Richmond covered the assassination of President Kennedy and was the lead criminal-courts reporter of the Jack Ruby murder trial. He has written for *People* magazine, *TIME*, and *Newsweek*, among other national magazines and daily newspapers. His 1995 book *SELENA!* was a number-one *New York Times* best-seller.